THANKS ELBOW A BLESSING

BLESSED WITH BIPOLAR

36 God-Given Gifts of Manic-Depression

[signature]
8/7/09

Richard H. Jarzynka
(Ya'Zhynka)

Copyright © 2009
by Richard H. Jarzynka (Ya'Zhynka)

Blessed With Bipolar
36 God-Given Gifts of Manic-Depression
by Richard H. Jarzynka (Ya'Zhynka)

Printed in the United States of America

ISBN 978-1-60791-888-2

All rights reserved solely by the author. The author guarantees all contents are original and do not infringe upon the legal rights of any other person or work. No part of this book may be reproduced in any form without the permission of the author. The views expressed in this book are not necessarily those of the publisher.

Unless otherwise indicated, Bible quotations are taken from The Holy Bible, New International Version of the Bible, Copyright © 1973, 1978, 1984 by International Bible Society, Used by permission of Zondervan, and The NLT, Holy Bible, New Living Translation, Copyright © 1996 Used by permission of Tyndale House Publishers, Inc., Wheaton, Illinois 60189, and The "New American Bible" taken from *"Reading God's Word, Daily Mass Readings, Church Year A 2005*, Copyright © 2004 by Living Faith Publications, Creative Communications for the Parish, Published by authority of the Committee on the Liturgy, United States Conference of Catholic Bishops, and "The Jerusalem Bible" taken from The Jerusalem Bible, Copyright © 1966, 1967, 1968 by Darton, Longman, and Todd, Ltd., and Doubleday & Company, Inc., and

"The Message, paraphrase" taken from *The Message*, Copyright © 1993, 1994, 1995, 1996, 2000, 2001, 2002 Used by permission of NavPress Publishing Group, and The CEV, Contemporary English Version, Copyright © 1995 by American Bible Society, and The KJV, King James Version, 1987 printing, and *The One Year Bible, New Living Translation*, Copyright © 1985, 1986, 1987, 1989, 1991 by Tyndale House Publishers, Inc.

Front Cover Sketch by Janet Cruz

www.xulonpress.com

TABLE OF CONTENTS

1. AMAZING EXTREMES 9
2. HEARING VOICES 17
3. GOD IS NOT SCREWING WITH YOU 25
4. HAVING BIPOLAR vs. BEING BIPOLAR 39
5. A FIGHTING SPIRIT 43
6. A REASON TO LIVE 53
7. FAITH THAT MAKES WORKS COME ALIVE 81
8. NOTES FROM THE NUTHOUSE 87
9. DELUSIONS OF GRANDEUR 101
10. "... A METHOD WHICH REPEATEDLY FAILS MAY POSSIBLY BE WRONG" 115
11. MESSING UP EVERYTHING 121
12. MEDS vs. BOOZE 125
13. GUILT AND THE PRESENCE OF GOD 131
14. "DEALING WITH" AUTHORITY 139
15. FORGIVENESS 157
16. OPERATION SHUTDOWN 169
17. BONE-BREAKING BLESSINGS 177

18. COMFORTING WITH THE COMFORT
    GIVEN 187
19. THE CRAZINESS OF CHRISTIANITY 203
20. RESEARCH STUDIES 211
21. THIS TOO SHALL PASS............................219
22. SOCIAL SECURITY DISABILITY
    INCOME...225
23. IMPULSIVITY 233
24. GOD, GAYS, AND A GOOF-BALL'S
    BRAIN 243
25. BONE-BREAKING BLESSINGS,
    PART II 251
26. A TIME FOR MADNESS 255
27. BIPOLAR BOLDNESS................................261
28. GOD LIKES THE CRAZY PEOPLE...........301
29. A ONE-MAN DEBATE................................307
30. RACING THOUGHTS.................................319
31. BIPOLAR DIARY, MEDICATION..............323
32. LOUSY vs. PSYCH-WARD LOUSY...........329
33. ACCEPTING GIFTS 331
34. BIPOLAR, BUT SINGLE-HEARTED.........335
35. COMFORTING WITH THE COMFORT
    GIVEN, PART II.....................................347
36. NO END IN SIGHT......................................355
    About the Author *365*
    Endnotes...*367*
    Bibliography *369*

To my parents,

When anybody in their right mind would have long-since forsaken me,
You chose to love me even more.
Your love is how I know that God's love
Is the love of a Father.

CHAPTER 1

AMAZING EXTREMES

I cracked up – for the first time - on June 4, 1988, three weeks short of completing my Masters degree in Psychology. Some would say I had a nervous breakdown. The psych ward doctors said it was major depression. I say that I saw just how evil my sin is in the eyes of God and it scared the hell out of me.

I cracked up, broke down, and de-pressed. I cobbled together some mad reality and blew a fuse. I despaired, decompensated, detached, and derailed. I lost my mind, never to be the same again. Thanks be to God! Praise to You, Lord Jesus Christ!

One year later, during my second tour of duty as a psych ward inpatient, I completed my Masters degree in Psychology, taking my final class on three hour passes from the hospital. I woke up in the psych ward, went to class at Duquesne University in Pittsburgh, and returned to the hospital for the rest of the day – and night. Now that's bipolar! Psych grad-student by day. Psych ward patient by night. Two weeks prior to completing my degree, I kicked, thrashed, wrestled, clawed, and bit – literally – to keep from being restrained. I ended up strapped to a bed with a thorazine needle in my arm.

On February 2, 1980, I signed a letter of intent to attend Georgia Tech on a full football scholarship. Six months later I left Atlanta, never to return.

I did not know it until years later, but I was steeped in depression from the time I checked in at Field dormitory for Georgia Tech's training camp until the day I boarded a red-eye flight back home. I was sad, scared, guilt-ridden, and disconcerted, all while trying to compete at a level of football bigger, faster, stronger, and more complex than any I had ever played.

The anguish over the decision to leave Georgia Tech did not get resolved for twenty years. It hurt. I had busted my butt since I was twelve years-old to earn that scholarship. But without treatment, without some understanding of the disorder that I did not then know I had, leaving, drinking, and/or cracking-up were my only options. Toughing it out would have resulted in all three.

Did I make the best choice by leaving Georgia Tech? Maybe not. A full-blown crack-up in 1980 might have speeded my recovery. It was going to happen sooner or later. Leaving Georgia Tech may have simply delayed my inevitable and necessary crack-up by eight years to the aforementioned 1988 hospitalization.

So why did I leave? Why did I throw away the profound opportunity of a full football scholarship? Why did I give up on my boyhood dream just as it was being realized?

Fear. No, not fear of college football or Georgia Tech or the streets of Atlanta. I was afraid, in 1980, to go face-to-face with myself - alone. I was afraid to deal then with the sin God moved me to confront in a psych ward eight years later.

In December 1999, I was granted a full-tuition, merit-based scholarship to attend St. Thomas University School of Law in Miami, Florida. On March 23, 2001 I was immediately expelled without a hearing, without due process, and without notice of any charges against me. It happened within hours of the Dean of the law school learning that I have bipolar disorder.[1]

St. Thomas University claimed to have received allegations that I had made threats against the school. I had not and never did.

Further, when I later represented myself in my federal lawsuit against St. Thomas,[2] there was no one to come forward to say that they had heard me make the alleged threats against the school.[3] In fact, the woman whom I expected to be the school's star witness against me filed an affidavit stating that I had never made any threats and that she had never alleged that I had made any threats. I lost anyway. I was a resident of Pennsylvania suing a Florida law school in a Florida Court.

I have looked at the above events, cried, cussed, and called it all a nightmare. A tale of wasted potential and opportunities blown to pieces. It is now a tale of God working in all things for the good of those who love Him (Romans 8:28); a tale of amazing blessing in the extremes. Blessings – all of it! The dizzy joy, the mad energy, the intensity in everything <u>and</u> the depression, despair, anger, failure, and lost opportunities. All of it – Blessing.

I don't like book introductions. I give them a quick look to see if they have anything to do with the alleged subject matter of the text. If it's a list of acknowledgments or irrelevancies, I pass. So out of respect for those who are spending their time and/or money to see if I have anything of value to say, (A tremendously humbling honor for me, by the way. Thank you.) I wanted to get right at it. But I do think this whole thing requires some upfront clarification. Thus, we have the "Explanation" in the hole left by the Introduction.

As you already know, I have bipolar disorder. And since seemingly everyone who has ever written about the condition has told the horror story of raging mood swings, crippling depression, agitated and angry uncontrollable energy, racing thoughts, bankrupting spending sprees, broken relationships, sex-catastrophes, and just about every other sordid human experience that could be blamed on an irascible mood, I thought I might write about how Jesus Christ has made this "disorder" into His amazing, awe-striking, abundant gift to me!

I am not going to let you wander and search for the theme of this book. Here it is right between the eyes: When I am weak, then I am strong. For God's strength is made perfect in my weakness and in all things (even manic-depression), He works for my good. (2 Corinthians 12:9-10, Romans 8:28)

Therefore, since everybody is almost always beset with some degree of suffering, I offer these good works of bipolar disorder that God has done in my life. I set forth these blessings of bipolar to encourage you to seek the good that God is doing in whatever hardship, weakness, or pain that you may be enduring.

Some of what I write in the following pages can be playful and even silly at times. But since 'silly' is derived from the Old English word *saelig*, meaning 'blessed,' a little playfulness does seem appropriate for a book entitled, <u>Blessed with Bipolar</u>. Please know, however, that I am not making light of bipolar disorder or any other pain that a person may be suffering.

I know personally the depths of the hell of manic-depression. I am not writing to deny that agony. I am writing to declare that, in spite of the hell and through the hell, God is doing a miraculous work in you. I know this because He used bipolar disorder to do a miraculous work in my life beyond anything I could have dreamed – or suffered. I truly now look at my experience of bipolar disorder and see it as a blessing. I want you to know that there is hope. And that His name is Jesus Christ. I pray in His Name that

He will empower you to one day see bipolar disorder as God's blessing upon your life.

I understand that if you are currently struggling with depression, this may sound like full-bore nonsense. In fact, if somebody had said these things to me during an episode of agitated depression, I may well have told him that it was a bunch of balderdash. (I would not have said "balderdash," but what I would have said could not have made it past Xulon Press – the Christian publisher of this book.) I would have told that person that he was nuts if he thought anything about bipolar could be a blessing – a gift from God. But that notion is no more crazy than this statement from one of the most brilliant men of all time:

". . . so I wouldn't get a big head, I was given the gift of a handicap to keep me in touch with my limitations. Satan's angel did his best to get me down; what he in fact did was push me to my knees. No danger then of walking around high and mighty! At first I didn't think of it as a gift, and begged God to remove it. Three times I did that, and then He told me, "My grace is enough; it's all you need." (2 Corinthians 12:7b-9a, The Message Paraphrase)

God will perfect His power in your weakness. Embrace Christ and His power will dwell in you. Ask, seek, and knock for the power of His Holy Spirit to explode within you. And keep on asking, seeking, and knocking (aggressively! with a little fire in your spirit, and with a heart expectantly overflowing with praise and thanksgiving for what God is about to do) until the Holy Spirit's power explodes throughout your life. And bipolar disorder will be a "a slight momentary affliction" preparing you "for an eternal weight of glory beyond all measure." (2 Corinthians 4:17)

CHAPTER 2

HEARING VOICES

The phrase, "God told me . . .," is often met with the response, "God . . . *told* you?!" and a look that says, "Are you getting enough thorazine?" I know that look, but when you have bipolar and you <u>do</u> take psychotropic medication, that look does not keep you from saying, "God told me . . ."

At the risk of seeming sane, I will now clearly state the obligatory disclaimer: "I have never heard the audible voice of God!" That might make me seem a little less crazy, however – just like everybody else – I do still "get told by God." Having bipolar disorder may make that easier for me to believe. I entertain some strange thoughts even when they are not from God. But there are times when He breaks in and I know that the words are not all coming from me.

I was writing long-hand in a notebook on August 21, 2007 about some plans and dreams I had for writing, preaching, and counseling. I was trying to figure out what sort of work God wanted me to do when the Holy Spirit piped up in my spirit and we had the following conversation. Since I was already writing, I was able to scribble it all down as we debated. It went something like this:

I had just copied into my notebook this statement written by Tony Dungy, Head Coach of the NFL's Indianapolis Colts, " . . . God uses the logic and the passion He has given us to help direct us." (Dungy, 2007, p.40)

That got me to thinking dangerously and I wrote down these questions for myself? "Is God asking me what *I* want to do, the kind of ministry *I want* to have? Is He saying, 'Decide what you want to do. Do it with all your heart, mind, soul, and strength in service to me, and I will bless you in it?"

"So," I asked myself, "What do I want to do?"

And I promptly answered:

- Write, "Blessed with Bipolar"
- Preach at churches throughout the country
- Private counseling practice

For some reason, Luke 13:22 then came to me and I wrote it down at the bottom of the page in my notebook:

"Jesus went through one town and village after another, teaching as He made his way to Jerusalem."

I started to ask myself another question. "What if –?" And bang! The Holy Spirit barged in and the next thing I wrote was, "What if's are questions that will keep you from ever committing to anything. What if you just trust me? I trust you to make a decision about your ministry. Now, trust me! Don't I love you enough to shut the door if you make an honest _bad_ decision with every desire and intention to do my will?"

"That's all I want," I said – and wrote, "To do your will. So, what is it?"

"First, you have to make that choice," He said and I wrote.

"Huh . . .? You'll tell me what you want me to do right – _after_ I decide what it is that you want me to do?"

"No. It's going to take a little more than that."

"A little more?" I raised my brow, quipped, and almost smirked. "Sounds – now I don't mean to offend you – but it all sounds a little upside-down. _You_ trusting _me_ to make a decision about _your_ will – which I still won't know – and then it takes a little more?"

"Well," said the Holy Spirit, "You still won't know. Not if you mean one-hundred percent certain. But you'll have more reason to believe."

"So, when do I get to know – like one-hundred percent certain?" I asked.

"Never.

"Never?!" I popped.

"Not on earth," He laughed. "What did you think faith meant? How could you have faith if you knew – like one-hundred percent certain?"

"Okay, that makes sense if faith means believing what you can't know one-hundred percent certain."

"Right."

"Right?!" I exclaimed. "You ever hear of Abbot and Costello?"

"Not only did I know Abbot and Costello," the Holy Spirit said, still laughing, "I knew *Who*."

I squinted, shook my head, and sighed.

"So, what's this 'a little more' I need to do after making the decision for my ministry before I get to know your will for the decision? I mean . . . before I get to have more reason to believe that maybe I am doing your will?"

"Now, you're getting it!" said the Holy Spirit.

"Third base?!?" I yelped. "I don't know what I'm talking about!"

"Be strong and courageous," He firmly quoted scripture, "Make a decision. Then take some action. Start working on the ministry."

"Sounds like you want to know that I'm serious."

"Not a bad idea, don'ch'ya think?" He winked and nodded.

"This ain't so easy." I said, feigning protest.

"Never said it would be."

"No," I sighed, "I can't say that you did."

"And you ain't seen nothin' yet."

"I figured," said I, laughing. "So, I make a decision. Take some action, and then you'll tell me if I got it right."

"Nope. You'll know without me saying a word whether you have more reason to believe that you're on the right track."

"And . . . what if I'm on the wrong track – wait! I know. 'What if' questions will keep me from ever doing anything."

"Yes!" He beamed. "That's my boy. You *are* getting it."

"So, I keep making decisions and taking action. Not knowing one-hundred percent if I'm right – until I get off my duff and do something and then I'll have a better idea," I pressed on with something sort of like confidence.

"That's right," He encouraged.

"And if I go too far down the wrong track, you'll throw up a road-block."

"See, I knew I could trust you," said God.

"*You* trust *me*?" I exclaimed, "Well, I guess it doesn't get any better than that."

"Sure it does," laughed the Lord.

"And you'll be guiding me all the way, right?"

"Man, I live inside of you!" He boomed with delight. "I've been guiding you even when you didn't know that you were being guided. That's what I've been trying to tell you."

"Won't the devil try to confuse me?"

"Who?" the Holy Spirit paused, "Oh, yeah, him. You let me handle him. Your job is to stick closer and closer to me. Live in my Word. Abide in Christ like the branch in the vine. And you'll have more and more reason to believe and make decisions and take action – with confidence – and with more of my power in you and behind you and going before you."

"You are a lamp unto my feet."

"Yes. Just don't get the idea that I'm going to light up the whole playing field all at once."

Now – seventeen months later – I have a publishing agreement with Xulon Press for "Blessed with Bipolar," I am two classes short of ministry certification, and I have some money available should I decide to rent a small office for a private counseling practice. All because my bipolar brain was willing to believe that God wanted to have a chat.

*"In the time of my confession
In the hour of my deepest need
When the pool of tears beneath my feet
Floods every newborn seed
There's a dying voice within me
Reaching out somewhere
Toiling in the danger
And in the morals of despair
Don't have the inclination
To look back on any mistake
Like Cain I now behold this chain
Of events that I must break
In the fury of the moment
I can see the Master's hand
In every leaf that trembles
And in every grain of sand."*

- Bob Dylan (1981)

CHAPTER 3

GOD IS NOT SCREWING WITH YOU

"Consider yourself kicked in the ass." Those were the words Pastor Bruce Edwards said to me in the sanctuary of Allison Park Church this morning – right after I went to him for prayer. I needed it, the kick more so than the prayer. And Bruce knew it. Thank God – and Bruce. His kick is the reason I am sitting here in front of the keyboard, forcing myself to type.

I had not been writing for the past three weeks. Writing half of a book does not cause it to finish itself. I needed to get moving and I knew it.

I went to Bruce at the close of the 9:00 AM service and told him that I had been doing some writing over the past year, but I had recently stalled out. I asked him to pray for me to get cranked up again, expecting him to burst forth with a full-fiery Pentecostal blizzard of petition. But Bruce had other ideas. He responded with, "Can I ask what you are writing about?"

Uh-oh. The ever-assertive Bruce wanted to do even more for me than pray. Fortunately, my bipolar nature is often willing to expose itself to danger in service of a potential greater good. And I trust Bruce. I trust him so much that I revealed to him several years ago that I have bipolar disorder while I was still struggling and likely to explode or despair at any moment. At the time, I was out of work, I had been expelled from law school, and I was in the midst of representing myself in the federal lawsuit I had brought against said school. You might say that Bruce has known me under less than ideal conditions. He is one of those people who has seen a glimpse of the ragingly hair-triggered-mood-swinging Ya'Zhynka and did not run away. In fact, he chose to get closer – sort of like Christ touching a leper.

When Bruce asked about the content of what I had been writing, I knew that he had my best interests at heart.

"I'm writing about bipolar disorder," I said. "How it's a blessing. How when we are weak, then we are strong and Christ's strength is made perfect in our weakness. Bipolar disorder has been a blessing to me, Bruce." His eyes burned steely into mine from six inches away and I knew he meant business.

"That story _needs_ to be told," he demanded, his eyes leaving no doubt, driving into mine, and his hands firmly grabbing and shaking my shoulders. He was Bill Cowher without the spit. "People need to hear that. People need to know that God isn't screwing with them." I felt his excitement and the fire was lit. My spirit yelled and punched its fists in the air. "Yes! Yes! Yes!" I knew that Bruce believed in my project. He believed in the ability God has given me. But . . . uh-oh . . . he wasn't finished.

"So what's keeping you from doing it?"

I shook my head. "I've just been lazy."

"Listen to me," Bruce insisted in a tone to which I often rebel, but, oh, how I listened. Whatever he had to say, I needed to hear it. I wanted to hear it. We stared straight at each other, his eyes still six inches from mine. God was up to something.

"You have a spirit of discipline. Put down the remote. Fast from whatever is keeping you from doing this and get it done! You are going to write today. I don't care if it's on the back of a napkin – you are going to write today. And on Wednesday you are going to show me what you've written between now and then. Send me an email. Do you have my email address?"

"Yes," I responded, revving to the challenge, and nearly simultaneously we both said, "Accountability."

Bruce pressed on, reminding me that when God allows us to go through a trial, He isn't doing it to get Himself some kicks. He is working in it for our good. He blesses us.

"Yes," I exclaimed. "And it's not just a blessing that comes after the trouble. There is blessing right in the middle of it. The trouble is a blessing."

Bruce nodded and laughed, "Consider yourself kicked in the ass." And only then did he pray, but after having had my ass so wonderfully kicked, I cannot recall the words. It doesn't matter. I knew he was talking to God and God was speaking through him.

Not only was I inspired to write, but I had made a commitment to a brother in Christ to write. And I knew he was going to hold me to it. Thank God – and Bruce.

The three shiftless weeks of not writing had been three of the best of my life. I had visited my sisters, brother-in-law (to whom I would rather refer as my brother), and my nephews (5 year-old Mowgli and 21 month Crash Cruz. Actually, Henry and Teddy Jack, but what good is an uncle if he doesn't have a nickname for his nephews). I spent a few days with them and then we traveled to Myrtle Beach, South Carolina (every Pittsburgher ends up there sometime) to meet my parents for what is becoming an annual week-long vacation. I then went back to Tennessee with my Confederate family and spent another week there. Magnificent. Every last minute of it. But I scarcely picked up a pen the entire time.

I thought about writing. I hoped to write. I planned to write, sort of. I even took my laptop with me. But that doesn't get it done. I kept telling myself, "We-e-e-l-l, I can't really expect to do any writing now. I'm spending time with my family." And, yes, spending time with my family is a wonderful, joyous, Godly thing for me to do. But I got lazy. I could have written during the vacation, but I made it an excuse not to put my mind and body (writing is physical) to the privilege God has given me. And the laziness had carried over for a week after I got back home.

Laziness is not a blessing, neither of bipolar disorder nor anything else.

"A little extra sleep, a little more slumber, a little folding of the hands to rest, and a half-written book does not finish itself." (Proverbs 24: 33, sort of)

I needed to get back to work and these several paragraphs are the start.

You may be nearly unconscious with depression, twitching with anxiety, or exploding like only bipolar rage can explode. In the words and boldness of Bruce Edwards, "Listen to me."

I am looking straight into your eyes and I have been right where you are – many times. "<u>God is not screwing with you</u>!"

Yes, you are hurting badly – and you have legitimate reasons to be frustrated, angry, and/or depressed. You feel a million miles from God. You may even doubt that He ever existed. I've been there, too – more times than I would like to admit. You may be angrily growling, "God! How could you do this to me?" You might have even cursed Him (Job did not curse God in the first chapter, but read the rest of his book. There's a whole lot of griping in there that is not directed at any human being). Maybe you are thinking that this time you have gone too far. That you've screwed up so badly that God will never take you back. I know from my own many personal experiences.

God knew that you were angry with Him before you did. He can handle it. God is holding your ranting-somber self in the palm of His hand right now. And I don't blame you one bit if you don't believe me.

If you are anything like me and you are now in severe emotional pain, you may have just thrown the book across the room. You don't want to hear even one more word of my "nonsense." But you are reading. You want to know that the hell you are going through makes some kind of agonizing sense. That there is an end to it. You might even have a dying, but not dead, smolder of hope that there is some good purpose in it.

It is not enough for me to point you to the Word of God and say, "When you are weak, then you are strong for God's strength is made perfect in your weakness." (2 Corinthians 12:9-10) It is true, but you are not close to feeling it right now. It is not enough for me to point you to the Word of God and say, "I know that in all things – even this excruciating pile of crap – God is at work for your good." (Romans 8: 28) It's easy for me to say that, but it's not enough. I need to show you that it is true.

Showing you that God blesses us in our trials and that our trials, themselves, can be blessings from Him is what this book is all about. I try to make that point in almost every chapter, but here I need to get specific. I need to write about a time when I believed that God was, indeed, screwing with me. A time when it was nearly impossible for me to believe any promise from Him other than salvation. It was not all that long ago.

I had been holding on for a couple of years and more to what I believed were promises from God.

The first was that I would be married. The second was that I would win the lawsuit.

I am trying to be as honest as possible about my failures, emotions, and embarrassments in this book, but I am not going to detail the blow-up of the marriage promise. No need to drag down the quasi-innocent. That's the convenient reason. The truth is that I really don't want to put myself through everything that would entail.

It will have to be sufficient for me to say that in one moment it became abundantly clear that the marriage promise was not going to happen. I had been convinced that I had been given the promise in and through scripture, the words of a Christian friend, dreams, preaching, and circumstances.

The promise blew up and I was hurt. And I was angry. Angry with the Person who made the promise and would not fulfill it. "God, you made this promise and I hung onto it like a fool for two years," I bitterly complained. "If you're not going to do this, how can I believe anything that I think you have said to me," I doubted, growling. "Maybe all I can believe is that Christ died to pay for my sins. That I'll go to heaven once you let this miserable life finally end."

Yes, that is honestly sometimes how I - the man writing a Christian book - talk to God. Honestly.

"God, if you're not going to give me this promise, then how can I believe your promise that I will win this lawsuit that has taken up five years of my life – while I waited for you to do something?"

Two months later, I lost my appeal in the Eleventh District Federal Circuit Court and the lawsuit was dead. The next step would have been the United States Supreme Court. But I needed to put an end to it.

I went to my computer late one night just before Christmas 2006 and found an email stating that the court had found against me. The judges did not write an opinion. They gave no reason for their finding, saying only that they concurred with the ruling of the United States District Court for the Southern District of Florida.

I didn't yell. I didn't fight. I didn't throw the computer or punch my fist through a wall. I went into shock. I was out of work and I had just lost a lawsuit that I had been fighting as my own attorney for four years.[2] A lawsuit that would have awarded me damages in the amount of the future wages I would have earned as an attorney – had I not been expelled. I was 44 years old, owed $39,000 in school loans, and had not had a full-time job in seven years. I had no bank account, no stocks, no 401(k), no investments, no insurance policies. The future had just dried up – in alleged contradiction of the promise of God.

I took 50 milligrams of seroquel for the first time in months and fell hard asleep, believing that God was screwing with me.

I woke up the next morning and did nothing and talked to no one. I didn't rant and roar, stomping through the house as my Dad surely must have expected. I was not even depressed. I sat shell-shocked all day to the background noise of Rush Limbaugh and Sean Hannity. I do not recall whether I prayed that night. If I did it was just enough to remind God and convince myself that I still believed.

The next morning started much the same. I buried my head in a cup of coffee and sat, lights out, at the kitchen table, staring into a plate of cheese and whatever was left from dinner, compelled to pick up pieces because eating is a habit.

And God moved simply, without my knowledge or permission.

"Dad!" I snapped, rising more quickly than I had in thirty-six hours. "I'm going to the mall. I'm not gonna sit here all day, comatose, again. I have to do something."

I surprised myself with that. When I'm that bipolar I usually stay "comatose" for three or four days.

I sleep-walked into Gloria Jean's, instinctively ordered my usual 32-ounce Sport Tea, and wandered dazed through Ross Park Mall, slowly recognizing that the outside world had not departed with the news of my lost federal appeal.

What I thought would never end was all over – suddenly. There would be no more writing Responses to Defendant's Written Interrogatories and Motions to Compel Production and Plaintiff's Third Amended Complaints. No more last minute re-reading cases that I knew inside-out and scrambling to the post office to keep the court from slamming my argument in its deadline. No more massive requests for documents and undisclosed subpoenas. No more fighting with opposing trial lawyers conditioned to the bending of ethics.

The second biggest fight of my life was over. I was bruised and scarred and beaten. I had brawled like a savage and lost. And Ross Park Mall bustled on with Christmas as if nothing had happened!

All around me I saw people going on with their lives and I sensed that **I** was still alive. The worst that I had imagined could happen had happened, but I was alive and drinking Sport Tea. I had no idea what to do next, but I was doing what I normally did, drinking Sport Tea and moving among the living.

God was moving simply.

As I drove home, the pressing, warring, rushing weight of five years lifted out of my brain. In all honesty, I had loved the fight and I felt a bit empty without it. I had spent hundreds upon hundreds of hours doing work I had no business doing. That, in itself, was the hand of God. I am not an attorney. There was something about it I would miss and, no doubt, I was crushed by the defeat. But I could breathe again. I had lost, but, after five years, I could breathe again.

I had been crushed, but not abandoned. God had been with me more intimately than ever for five years. And there had been miracles in the very heart of all the battling, research, writing, sorrow, anger, prayer, and persecution. Documents showing up on my doorstep at the precise moment I direly needed them and had no way of getting them. The law school's supposed 'star witness' calling me out of nowhere after three years and telling me that she would testify in my favor – at the very moment that I had given up all hope and was buried, mid-afternoon, in my bed. My lawyer Uncle impossibly calling me from his office when I had not spoken with him in weeks – seconds after I had angrily howled, "God has abandoned me," and dropped to my knees, "My God, why have you forsaken me?" My Uncle never calls me from his office, but for some Godly reason, at that very moment, the phone rang. And he had precisely the legal advice I needed.

The lawsuit was an intense and emotional struggle that, for five years, almost never left my head. And I ended up losing. So, was God screwing with me?

Over those five years I had prayed and praised and come to know God like never before. I joined Allison Park Church. I met wonderful, Godly people who listened to my story and loved me and prayed for me and with me. I was baptized in the Holy Spirit. Throughout the entire five years, God had been transforming me.

I lost the lawsuit and the alleged promise of marriage, but I had gained so much. I had seen my mother and father fighting desperately for me, willing to do anything to help. I watched God deliver my father from alcohol. I was 44 and my Dad was 66 and we traveled twelve-hundred miles together as warriors, brothers-in-arms, doing legal battle with a law school. Fighting a giant on the giant's home field, in the court of the giant's first cousin. How many 44 year-old men get to do that with their Dad? It was an honor to go down fighting in a blaze – with my Dad fighting right beside me! And then go goofy, leaving the courtroom and hurling my-screwball-self over and over into the ocean, cackling like a middle-aged kid while my grinning Old Man cheered me on. Yeah, we lost. And I'd do it again in a heartbeat.

After all of that how could I go on thinking that God was screwing with me? In all of that crap, He transformed me! Yes, my life was a mess for a long time, but God was not screwing with me and I would not trade one minute of it. Because of God's work in my nightmare, I am a better man today than I was seven-and-a-half years ago. And He was doing that work smack in the midst of the garbage. And I praise Him for it – the work and the garbage! And He will do the same in the midst of your garbage if you just don't let go of Him.

God did not break His promise to me. I got the promise wrong. God's real promise was better than anything I expected.

As I drove home from Ross Park Mall that partly sunny December day, I actually noticed the sun. And in the wake of my bitter legal defeat, I realized that I could still go out for a drive. I could still go to the gym and watch a football game. I still had friends. I could still take a walk in a beautiful park at no charge. I still had my wonderful, loving, amazing, supportive-beyond-all-reason family. I still had everything I need by the grace of God. Always did and always will. Hallelujah!

From that moment forward I have had more peace and joy than ever before. It was a moment I had expected would destroy me. But ever since that moment my peace and joy and intimacy with God just keeps growing. It continues to puzzle me. "How in the world can things be so good," I ask. And then I just enjoy it, still with very little money, unemployed, and abundantly unmarried.

Some would call me crazy.

"Anything outside of hell is amazing grace."
  - Mario Herrera

CHAPTER 4

HAVING BIPOLAR vs. BEING BIPOLAR

I have bipolar disorder. Bipolar disorder does <u>not</u> have me. Bipolar disorder is not, my identity. It is not who I am. Bipolar disorder impacts my personality, emotions, and behavior. It does not <u>*dictate*</u> what I think, believe, say, or do.

There are blessings that come with "having bipolar disorder." "Being bipolar," on the other hand, would be nothing but a burden.

If I think of myself as "being bipolar" (or of bipolar as being <u>*my*</u> being), then I am controlled by it. I cannot then be anything but bipolar. And not even I (who have embraced the benefits of having bipolar) want to be bipolar <u>*all*</u> of the time without any choice to ever be otherwise.

So, who is bipolar? The one who says, "I am bipolar."

And the one who 'has bipolar disorder' is the one who commands, "I have bipolar disorder, but it does NOT have me." It is a matter of how I choose to view myself in relation to the disorder.

This may seem like an inconsequential semantic distinction, but think of how powerful it is to say, "I am bipolar." What is that person actually saying? "I am this mental illness and this mental illness is me." "I am never not, and will never not, be this madness." Or, to take it a step further into defining oneself: "My entire identity is completely wrapped up in continuing to be bipolar disorder." Now, let's get extreme. How about this? "I am the living breathing, walking, talking, physical, mental, and spiritual personification of bipolar disorder."

To say, "I have bipolar disorder," however, is to say: "Yes, I do have this mental and emotional trait about me that is different than what most people experience. A lot of it is a real challenge and has made life very difficult for periods of time (some long periods of time), but I have found that there are some things about this condition that do benefit me. Yes, it is a challenge that may always be in my life, but I can deal with it. I can be successful. It does _not_ control what I think, what I believe, what I say, or what I do."

Bipolar disorder is an unavoidable fact of my experience. I have it. It is a part of my life – everyday of my life. But my identity (the person whom I am _never not_) is who I am in Jesus Christ.

When I take bipolar disorder and its impact on my personality, thinking, and behavior and submit it to Christ, bipolar disorder is transformed. The Holy Spirit transforms the disorder and He transforms me. He, in His infinite wisdom and power, has used the disorder as He uses all things – to make me more like Christ.

If I say, "I *am* bipolar disorder," then I cannot take control of it and surrender it to Christ. If I *have* bipolar disorder, then I can do anything I want with it. I have *it*. It does **NOT** have me!

*"I've always been different
with one foot over the line
winding up somewhere
one step ahead or behind
It ain't been so easy
but I guess I shouldn't complain
I've always been crazy
but it's kept me from goin' insane"*
        - Waylon Jennings (1978)

CHAPTER 5

A FIGHTING SPIRIT

I am a sinner. In fact, there has not been one day in my life when I have not sinned in either word, thought, or deed. And when I consider that Jesus said that if you have lusted in your heart you have already committed adultery and that if you are angry with your brother, it is as though you have committed murder, then on most days I have sinned many times. I am not proud of it. I am confessing it right up front so you know where I stand and that I am not among the 'holier than thou.'

If I were not a sinner, I would have no need of Jesus. My sinless, perfect life would earn me a place in heaven. Since that is not the case, I need the sinless life of Jesus and his crucifixion to pay the penalty for my sin and ransom me from the hell that I so deserve. And by hell I mean eternal separation from God. That's bad. When I consider that every – <u>EVERY</u> – good thing that I have is a gift from God that I do not deserve, then being eternally separated from Him means never again having any good thing.

So why did I need to go into all of that? Because I am going to talk about some times when my words and deeds have not been very Christlike. Let it be known that I confess that from the start.

God put a good fighting spirit in every man. (Eldredge, 2001, pp. 10, 11, 19-38, 141) He was not surprised when the serpent tempted Adam. When God put Adam on earth, He knew that evil would be right there with him. In fact, God allowed the serpent to tempt Adam.

That may not sit well with some. But you cannot deny that if God had simply whispered, "No," the serpent would have kept his mouth shut. Now don't get the idea that I am saying that God approved of Adam's sin or even accepted it as Adam "only being human." God gave Adam the ability to resist the devil and flee temptation. God gave Adam a good fighting spirit. Adam failed to use it. (Eldredge, 2001, pp. 48-52)

I, too, have, at times, failed to use my good fighting spirit when it was desperately needed. I have also distorted it and used it destructively.

Scripture commands us not to sin in our anger. (Ephesians 4:26) I have not only sinned in anger, I have sinned in fits of bipolar rage. But sinning in anger can also mean quietly manipulating somebody or calmly making a pseudo-innocent remark that cuts another to the core. I would rather have my anger out in the open where I can deal with it than bury it so deep that I don't recognize the passive-aggressive harm I am doing all around me. Bipolar has forced me to see my anger, start dealing with it, and get to know the good fighting spirit with which God has blessed me.

There is a story from my father's childhood that he has told me a couple of times. My father's mother died in 1942 prior to my dad's third birthday. That meant that his upbringing was sometimes unlike that of the average child. (There has also never been another mind bent quite like his, but that has nothing to do with my grandmother's passing.)

Most of my Dad's relatives lived in the same neighborhood – the Polish Hill section of Pittsburgh. But there were times, simply as a result of the circumstances, that he ended up in some odd places for a youngster. One of those places was the Polish Hill Veterans of Foreign Wars Club on Brereton Avenue. A beer hall. The kind of place you find on half the blocks of every neighborhood in Pittsburgh. That VFW, circa 1948, is the setting for my father's story.

My Dad was somewhere between five and ten years-old. I would imagine that in 1948 nobody gave a second thought to a child hanging around a bar like that VFW. My Dad was there with his grandfather, John Jarzynka, Sr., and his father, Hank. They were playing poker with some other men. I doubt that any of them were near sober. And, as sometimes happens while playing poker under the influence, the men had a . . . "disagreement." One half-drunk accused another half-drunk of cheating or lying or some other who-knows-what non-sense and one of the younger men raised his voice to John Jarzynka (my great-grandfather who, in the pictures I've seen, looked ready for a fight) and yapped, "If you were twenty years younger, I'd kick your ass."

Hank Jarzynka (my grandfather) jumped to his feet and snarled, "I am twenty years younger!" He punched the man in the mouth and sent him under a table. I knew my grandfather and I don't doubt my father's story. And, having spent a number of my younger days on Polish Hill, I assume that the men from that barroom all saw each other the next Sunday morning at Immaculate Heart of Mary Roman Catholic church, just a few doors down from the VFW.

When I first heard that story, I dreamed of reliving it someday.

My grandfather likely could have defended his father without throwing that punch. But when you're a young boy and you hear that kind of story about your grandfather, you want to be just like him. There's something in a boy that loves a good fight – especially a fight for something so noble as defending your Dad. And, though my grandfather may well have sinned in throwing that punch, I do believe God has put a "fighting spirit" in the soul of every man. (Eldredge, 2001, pp10,11,19-38,141)

Because of bipolar disorder I have been forced to learn to deal with that fighting spirit. It has gone through some trial and error. That's why I started this chapter by confessing my sin. I have no desire to glorify it and I will not attempt to justify it. But I do know that God can, and does, use our errors to mold us into the men He calls us to be.

More than fifty years after "The Punch" that happened 15 or so years before my birth, I sat in a high school football stadium with my father who was 63 at the time – just about my great-grandfather's age on the night of "The Punch." I didn't care much about the game. I was there to see my niece play the flute in the high school band at half-time. But the home team was taking the worst beating I had ever seen and my father kept up a running commentary on every dimension of their incompetence.

I noticed a man about my age in the bleacher row in front of us twitching and turning as my Dad volunteered his color commentary. The man did not look pleased. I assumed that he had a kid out there on the wrong end of the slaughter. My Dad was not being malicious and he was not bellowing out loud. He was just giving me his honest, critical analysis of what he was watching fall apart on the field. The fact that he was dead-on accurate did not make the man in front of us any more pleasantly disposed. But I figured that my Dad had a right to his opinion and if the guy in front of us didn't like it, well, the place wasn't sold out. He could have found another seat somewhere out of earshot.

As the game hit halftime, the man in front of us shook his head and snapped up out of his seat. When he got to the stairs, he pointed angrily at my father, sneered, and told him that he wanted to see him in the stadium concourse. That was not good. My Dad had no idea what was going on, but he is not one to back away from another man's angry confrontation. He was in that barroom on Polish Hill more than fifty years ago and he is no slight figure. He is 6 feet tall and at the time weighed about 270 rock-solid, broad-backed, and big-bellied pounds built on Iron City Beer, hard work, and a lifetime of homemade stuffed cabbage, Polska kielbasa, and just about everything else that would curl the hair of the American Heart Association. My Dad lifted himself up and stepped out to meet the man's challenge.

The world will never know how my 63-year-old Dad would have fared. He had a bipolar son sitting next to him and I heard the snarl of my grandfather echo-growling my inheritance down the beer-halls of half-a-century, "I am twenty years younger!"

When that 40-some-year-old man challenged my father he stepped onto the fighting side of manic-depression. I shot out of my seat and sprinted across the bleachers, suddenly wild with all impulse. I went instantly – _instantly_ – from mild-mannered spectator, waiting to see his niece play flute, to rabid bipolar standing up for his old man, violently, if necessary.

When I got to the top of the bleachers and saw that man glaring at my father, I leaped between them, wild-eyed and six inches taller than normal, roaring with a fist in the air, "You called out a 63-year-old man and you ended up with me! Now what are you gonna do about it?!" My teeth clenched and I blazed.

He stuttered, "I didn't call him out."

"Don't gimme that crap," I demanded. "He's 63-years-old and you challenged him to meet you up here. You got somethin' to say, say it to me. You're not gonna get to him!"

The man backed away and a middle-aged woman accused me of being drunk. A kid about 17 told me that his friends had me surrounded and I growled in his face, "Bring it!" A police officer approached and I walked directly over to him and said, "A man my age challenged my father to a fight and I wasn't about to let him do it . . . And now I'm gettin' outta here." I went to my car and drove off.

When I got home my mother was upset. She had witnessed the incident and was not happy with me. We talked briefly and I assured her, saying, "Mom, I promise you . . . if anything like that ever happens again . . . I will do the exact same thing." My old man laughed and it was pretty much over.

Many Christians, I suppose, would say that I sinned in my anger. Not that the anger itself was sin, but that it led me to do things that were sinful. I am sure that I could have handled the situation better, but I am also sure that when Jesus said, "Turn the other cheek," He was not telling us that we cannot defend our families.

I went too far, but I am pleased that I have that kind of fighting spirit. It is a dangerous trait of bipolar disorder, but it's not all bad. I am not saying that a Christian man should be out leaping into fist-fights at the drop of every hint of a possible insult. What I am saying is that this world is in a filthy moral, political, and interpersonal condition and it is the responsibility of every Christian man to have the guts to stand up and speak out against it.

I pray for the grace to harness that fighting spirit to the will of God, to be used only for His glory and never in sin. It is not easy.

The good fighting spirit is a fire that is somewhere in every man and is made to be used for good. (Eldredge, 2001, pp. 10, 11, 19-38, 141) Because of bipolar disorder, for better _and_ worse, I have had to deal with it more than most. But if I denied it, I would betray the man God made me to be. And without it, I would be useless. "God, direct this good fighting spirit that you gave me. Direct it to be used for your purposes, Lord."

Note: A couple of weeks after I finished writing this chapter, my two-year-old nephew, Teddy Jack, had sand thrown in his face by a five-year-old. When his brother, my six-year-old nephew, Mowgli (a.k.a. Hip-Cat Henry), heard what had happened, he said to his Mom, "You should have told him that you have a kid who is really hard to kill and He's gonna pound you like a brick." I guess it runs in the family. The kid knows intrinsically that God would want him to stand up strong for his family. And God gave him the good fighting spirit to do it

*"Ill that He blesses is our good
And unblest good is ill;
And all is right that seems most wrong,
If it be His sweet will."*

"I Worship Thee, Most Gracious God"
  - Frederick W. Faber (1849)

CHAPTER 6

A REASON TO LIVE

Abraham Biggs died on November 20, 2008 and he is demanding an answer from me. In my heart I can hear him asking, "How dare you call bipolar a blessing?"

Hours before he died, Abraham Biggs went online at Justin.TV and wrote the following blog post:

> "I hate myself and I hate living . . . I have let everyone down and I feel as though I will never change or never improve.
>
> "I am in love with a girl and I know that I am not good enough for her. I have come to believe that my life has all been meaningless. I keep trying and I keep failing. I have thought about and attempted suicide many times in the past." (Friedman, Nov. 21, 2008, ABC News)

I look at the words Abraham wrote on that blog and I know that twenty years ago I could have written every one of them except, "I . . . have attempted suicide many times in the past."

While he was blogging, Abraham linked to the internet a live web-cam video of himself in his room. After twelve hours of blog exchanges, Abraham Biggs took a mixture of opiates and benzodiazapene and committed suicide – while an untold number of people watched live on the internet. Abraham Biggs had bipolar disorder. (Friedman, Nov. 20, 2008, ABC News)

"Blessed?! You piece of garbage. This is agony!" I would growl out loud with rage if I saw a book titled Blessed with Bipolar while in the throes of an episode of anger, depression, and agitation. I can feel myself getting angry about it right now. As I write, my teeth are clenched, I am holding my pen inside a balled-up fist, and I'm deep-breathing down to my belly. My eyes are wide open and staring. Right now, this very moment, I am fighting-mad about the thought of bipolar disorder being a blessing. And I am not in the midst of an episode. I am merely thinking of how I would feel if I were in the midst of an episode and I saw the title of my own book. I would throw it across the room and curse myself. My pen is nearly punching through the paper right now.

"How could I make such a statement?" I demand of myself. "You know the agony. You know how people are suffering. You know the cross this madness is for them. How do you tell them it's a blessing?"

On June 4, 1988, I went to the psychiatric emergency room of St. Francis Hospital in Pittsburgh because I just could not bring myself to attempt suicide. I had planned the previous evening to wait until the middle of the night – when my parents, sisters, and brother would be sleeping – sneak out of the house with a fifth of whatever whiskey I could find and my entire prescription for elavil, an antidepressant. I would go to the end of our street, walk into the woods, sit down by the creek, drink half the fifth of whiskey, swallow the pills, and finish the whiskey while I waited to die. I wanted to put an end to that damnable, constant thunderstorm in my brain. The thunderstorm of fear, raging-panic, depression, and, now, madness.

I could not do it. I got up in the middle of the night, shaking wildly out-of-control and screaming. My mind was gone. I looked at the clock in my sisters' room and thought, "It doesn't matter what time it is. This is never going to end. This is what you deserve. The just-punishments of God."

But I could not do it. Something kept me from even going downstairs to the medicine cabinet to get the pills. (My brother later told me that I would not have made it out of the house. He knew the condition I was in and he kept himself awake all night because he knew that he might have to stop me.)

I went to the hospital the next morning with my only hope being that the doctors might drug me into oblivion and I could live out the rest of my days without having to think.

I cannot imagine anyone being in more emotional agony than I was when I planned to overdose on whiskey and elavil – but Abraham Biggs suffered an even more horrific living nightmare. And one day after his suicide, I hear him demanding of me, "How dare you call bipolar a blessing?"

There may have been times when Abraham experienced some of the blessings of bipolar – the exhilarating, hypo-manic energy that helps you get things done, the racing thoughts that – when harnessed – can bring a wondrous surge of creativity, the joy of being deeply touched by another's heartfelt emotion, the capacity to honestly know, admit, and express one's feelings, and a number of others that I will later discuss. But even if Abraham experienced those blessings in abundance, it still does not answer the question that is nagging me. "What about the suffering? Where is the blessing in that hell?"

It is a question that deserves to be answered.

Viktor Frankl was a Jewish psychiatrist imprisoned for three years in Nazi concentration camps at Auschwitz, Dachau, and elsewhere. (Frankl, 1984, About the Author) He survived to write about what empowered him to endure the unimaginable suffering that he witnessed and experienced. (Frankl, 1984)

Dr. Frankl wrote:

"We must never forget that we may also find meaning in life even when confronted with a hopeless situation, when facing a fate that cannot be changed. For what then matters is to bear witness to the uniquely human potential at its best, which is to transform a personal tragedy into a triumph, to turn one's predicament into a human achievement. When we are no longer able to change a situation – just think of an incurable disease such as inoperable cancer – we are challenged to change ourselves . . .

". . . In some way, suffering ceases to be suffering at the moment it finds a meaning, such as the meaning of a sacrifice." (Frankl, 1984, p.135)

I agree with Dr. Frankl. There is meaning in all suffering, value in all life no matter the suffering, and always a reason to keep on living. At the very least, the suffering is an opportunity to *fight* "to bear witness to the uniquely human potential at its best . . . to transform a personal tragedy into a triumph." (Frankl, 1984, p.135). That fight matters – even if the suffering never ends. It gives the suffering human being an almost supernatural reason to courageously go on.

The death by suicide of Abraham Biggs is a tragedy and it hurts me. At the moment he went online that last time, he had no way of knowing how good his life could be. He had no way of understanding how good *he* could be. I have been there. I know that the bio-chemical make-up of Abraham's brain, at that moment, would not allow him to see the full truth about himself and his life. At that moment, I believe it was bio-chemically impossible for him to see anything the least bit good about himself. I have been there, too – many times. The people close to him could have pored through lists of wonderful, self-sacrificing things he had done and his brain – the way it was chemically functioning in that moment – would have denied and rejected the facts of his "goodness" that were undeniably clear to all who knew him.

The death of Abraham Biggs is a tragedy. I am convinced that there was love and meaning in his life and that it would have grown. I am convinced that those close to him did not feel that he had – as he wrote – "let everyone down" (Abraham was only 19 years-old. He was far too young to have failed. If you're still breathing there is always another second chance.) To the contrary, I believe those close to him saw his struggle and admired the way he would "keep trying." There certainly could have been profound meaning in that for him and them.

I am certain that there were many times in Abraham's 19 years when he triumphed over the pain of bipolar disorder. The fact that he was in college at the time of his suicide is definitive proof of that. There is no doubt in my mind that he must have had to press through many awful bipolar episodes just to finish high school.

Many people who have bipolar turn to drugs and alcohol to obscure the pain rather than trying to find a way to press through it. Abraham could have taken that route, but instead, as he wrote, he would "keep trying." He would not have been in college if he had given up. And, as one who has bipolar, I am sure there were many prior opportunities for him to have given up– and with good reason. The suffering can, indeed, be hell.

Yes, Abraham Biggs committed suicide when the pain became unbearable and the disorder so distorted his thinking that he could not see anything good. But for 19 years he did press on and I believe he fought the good fight on a field that was more than slightly tilted against him.

I never met Abraham, but in his words I sense the tenderness of his heart – and strength. No, I do not think that suicide is in any way a demonstration of strength. But I read the words of this young man, knowing that he was in pure agony. Yet, at such a desperate moment, he was not complaining that life had treated him unfairly. He was lamenting in the belief that he had not been the kind of person that he thought he should have been.

It is certainly part true that Abraham was not the person he should have been; and part false. None of us is entirely the person we ought to be. But just his awareness that there was more to who he could be tells me that Abraham had made some progress toward getting there.

It seems that when Abraham wrote about his failures he was not talking about money or a lack of possessions and accomplishments. He was concerned that he had "let down" those who were close to him, that he was not "good enough" to love someone and be loved, and that he had not made anything "meaningful" out of his life. It takes strength for a man to openly express that kind of hurt and tenderness. Many never find the courage. Abraham did.

In his last despairing moments, Abraham Biggs was desperately trying to make some sense out of his life, to believe that he could be the loving person that he thought he not yet was – and wanted to be. He wanted, still, to find a reason to live. He would not otherwise have gone online. He would have taken the pills and been done with it without anyone having a clue. I am convinced that he fought until the end. I am convinced because I know from personal experience the challenge that he faced. This last crash into bipolar depression had severely distorted his perceptions and thinking.

When I think of Viktor Frankl's statement that "In some ways, suffering ceases to be suffering the moment it finds a meaning," (Frankl, 1984, p.135) I wonder what meaning Abraham Biggs could have found in his suffering with bipolar disorder and how that meaning might have caused the suffering to cease. (And whether that meaning is a blessing that makes the suffering worth enduring).

After I filed my lawsuit against the school that had expelled me, there were strange accusations brought against me, many legal challenges to which I was obligated to respond, much work to be done, and a good bit of bipolar suffering. I railed out loud when the school's attorney tried to make my Christian faith seem insane by stating that I claimed to be "on a divine mission to save the soul" of a law professor. (I did say it – only half in jest – but aren't we, as

Christians, to be on a divine mission to save all the souls around us by bringing them to Christ?)

The challenges of the lawsuit did spur episodes of rage and depression over the course of 50 months worth of litigation. But when I remembered that I was fighting with everything within my power – and God's - against what I believed to be a grave injustice, "the suffering ceased to be suffering." (Frankl, 1984, p.135) The fight itself gave the suffering "meaning." The fight itself made the suffering a blessing. I was able to press on in the power of the Holy Spirit. And I learned that not every blessing is a warm-fuzzy.

Abraham Biggs may have never experienced his struggle with bipolar as a blessing. It is hard to imagine that he could have 'felt' blessed in the midst of a manic-depressive episode. I do not deny his agony and I refuse to minimize it. It was worse than any I have known. But there was meaning in his struggle to live with and overcome that agony. And I believe there had to have been many times when he did overcome it, times when, in Dr. Frankl's words, Abraham did "bear witnesss to the uniquely human potential at its best." Times when he did "turn (his) predicament into a human achievement." (Frankl, 1984, p.135)

Abraham Biggs faced a powerful challenge in his life that – if he was anything like me – I am sure he would have chosen not to have. But we who have bipolar disorder do not have that choice. What we do have, however, is the opportunity to choose to face the challenge courageously and fight it out – even if just for the sake of not letting it win. That courage and that fight is a hard and sometimes painful blessing that is there for everyone who has bipolar disorder. You have a challenge that most do not face and an opportunity to make it a blessing. Make it a blessing! That *is* within our power to choose.

The struggle, itself – the challenge of the pain – gives life meaning. (Or, more specifically, how we choose to face the pain gives life meaning.) Enduring courageously is enough of a reason to keep on living. We may be overwhelmingly depressed as a result of bio-chemical processes in our brain, but we can still choose to love. Take it as a challenge. Make it a blessing. (Maybe that is the key. Maybe we must make the suffering a blessing – even if sometimes that means nothing more than enduring.) And do NOT try to do it yourself. Turn to God, see a doctor, get help. You have been called to take on a tremendous challenge. It is not going to go away. Fight it and force the blessings from it!

For we who are Christians, there is, of course, a far greater meaning in those times when bipolar disorder causes us some light and temporary affliction. (2 Cor. 4:17)

In order to better explain my thinking, it may be best to first list some of the many scripture passages that deal with suffering:

"But those who suffer he delivers in their suffering; he speaks to them in their affliction." Job 36:15

"For just as the sufferings of Christ flow over into our lives, so also through Christ our comfort overflows. If we are distressed, it is for your comfort and salvation; if we are comforted, it is for your comfort, which produces in you patient endurance of the same sufferings we suffer. And our hope for you is firm, because we know that just as you share in our sufferings, so also you share in our comfort." 2 Corinthians 1:5-7.

"He (Jesus) then began to teach them that the Son of Man must suffer many things and be rejected by the elders, chief priests and teachers of the law, and that he must be killed and after three days rise again." Mark 8:31.

"Dear friends, do not be surprised at the painful trial you are suffering, as though something strange were happening to you. But rejoice that you participate in the sufferings of Christ, so that you may be overjoyed when his glory is revealed. If you are insulted because of the name of Christ, you are blessed, for the Spirit of glory and of God rests on you." 1Peter 4:12-14.

"However, if you suffer as a Christian, do not be ashamed, but praise God that you bear that name." 1Peter 4:16

"In bringing many sons to glory, it was fitting that God, for whom and through whom everything exists, should make the author of their salvation perfect through suffering." Hebrews 2:10

"Because he (Jesus) himself suffered when he was tempted, he is able to help those who are being tempted." Hebrews 2:18.

"Therefore, since we have been justified through faith, we have peace with God through our Lord Jesus Christ, through whom we have gained access by faith into this grace in which we now stand. And we rejoice in the hope of the glory of God. Not only so, **but we also rejoice in our sufferings**, because we know that suffering produces perseverance; perseverance, character; and character, hope; And hope does not disappoint us because we know that God has poured out his love into our hearts by the Holy Spirt, whom he has given us." (**emphasis added**) Romans 5:1-5.

"For our light and momentary troubles are achieving for us an eternal glory that far outweighs them all." 2Corinthians 4:17

Again, I don't mean to deny or minimize anybody's suffering, but, in light of the above verses, suffering as a Christian does not sound like such a rotten deal. Look at the blessings that are gained when we join our sufferings to those of Christ.

God delivers us and speaks to us. (Job 36:15) Our comfort overflows and we are used to comfort others in their pain and bring them to salvation. (2 Corinthians 1:5-6) We are used to produce patient endurance in others. (2 Corinthians 1:7) We will be overjoyed when Christ's glory is revealed. (1 Peter 4:13) The Spirit of glory and of God rests on us. (1Peter 4:14) We gain perseverance, character, and hope. We rejoice in the midst of suffering. (Romans 5:3-4) We achieve an eternal glory that far outweighs all the suffering. (2 Corinthians 4:17).

When we remember all that God has promised to do in and through our suffering, how can we not see meaning in our trials. We are being conformed to the character of Christ, used of Him for His glory and to win souls to Him, and given the chance to share His glory. When we focus our minds and hearts on those purposes that God has in our suffering, does it not, somehow, at least in part, cease to be suffering? (Frankl, 1984, p. 135).

What was the meaning in Christ's suffering? I do not have a doctorate in theology, but I think I can take a shot at that one. I am certain that there are many biblical meanings in Christ's suffering, but there is none greater than the fact that He was the sinless Son of God who became man in order to suffer the death penalty in payment for the sins of man and bring the world to eternal salvation. Obviously, there could be no more noble-glorious meaning than that in any suffering. I would guess that saving the world is meaning enough to make almost any suffering worth eduring – if you must. But He could have easily avoided it.

I can almost hear you thinking that there is really nothing new in what I said in the last paragraph. But what has my mind revving is the possibility that maybe our sufferings can have the same meaning. Any trials that we endure can be used by God in the power of His Holy Spirit within us to win souls to Christ – if we suffer them well. Is it not possible that an unbeliever could look at us in our pain and say, "How can he go through this without lashing out, without throwing in the towel? Where does he get that joy? How can he still get down on his knees and praise God?" And that gives us the chance to tell them. How much would your suffering be worth if, joined to the sufferings of Christ, it kept one soul from an eternity in hell. The Bible tells us that one soul is worth more than all the world. Could a Christ-like endurance of your trials actually be worth more than all the world? If that could be the case, your suffering would not merely, somehow, cease to be suffering, it would be triumphant . . . noble . . . glorious.

There are biblical examples of Christ-like endurance of suffering that won souls to Jesus.

Paul and Silas sang praises to God while chained in prison. Their jailer and his family were saved and Paul and Silas were released. (Acts 16:16-40)

When Stephen praised God while being stoned to death for preaching Christ, it had to make at least some people wonder who this Jesus really was. What did the apostle Paul think when he heard Stephen's dying words, "Lord Jesus, receive my spirit . . . Lord, do not hold this sin against them." (Acts 7:54-8:1a) Could that image have stayed with Paul until he was struck down on the road to Damascus and brought face-to-face with the risen Christ?

I am sure that I have not exhausted the scriptural meanings that we can find in our suffering, but I do have a few to list here that I hope will be helpful.

Being Conformed to the Character of Christ

In times of trouble, we easily and happily recall Romans 8:28: "We know that in all things God works for the good of those who love Him." But we can just as easily forget what the Lord says in the very next verse: "For God knew his people in advance, and he chose them to become like his Son . . ." (Romans 8:29 New Living Translation)

So, when we look at the two verses in light of each other, we see that the promise of God to be constantly at work for our good means that in all things He is working to conform us to the character of Christ. I don't know about you, but sometimes I don't much like the process of being conformed to that which I am not. In fact, I sometimes fight it like a mad dog (just ask any of my former employers). But I am learning to submit because I do want to become more and more like Christ. Nobody ever said that process was going to be smooth like a rhapsody. At times, it means going through a painful trial. My pride has never given up easily. I could not let it go simply because it seemed like a good idea. It had to be beaten out of me. But that is what I signed up for when I willingly chose to nail my sins to the Cross of Christ.

The apostle Paul knew first-hand what he was talking about when he wrote that God is at work in all things . . . to conform us to the character of Christ. Even after being "caught up into paradise and (hearing) things so astounding they cannot be told," (2 Corinthians 12:4b, NLT) Paul was still not fully conformed to the character of Christ. He tells us that God still had to take the hammer and chisel to him to break his tendency toward pride. Paul writes that after receiving the astounding visions and revelations, he was given a thorn in the flesh to keep him from getting puffed up, a messenger from satan to torment him and keep him from getting proud. (2Corinthians 12:7b)

Let us not make the mistake of thinking that Paul's thorn was some light and brief nuisance that easily conformed him to the humbleness of Christ's character. Take a good look at 2Corinthians 12:7b. Paul describes his thorn in the flesh as _torment_, suffered at the hands of satan. And so as to keep us from getting the idea that God made that torment easy to endure, Paul writes, "Three different times I begged the Lord to take it away. Each time he said, 'My gracious favor is all you need. My power works best in your weakness." (2Corinthians 12:8-9a, NLT) Paul does not say that he politely _asked_ God to take away the thorn. He **begged** – three times!

Everything I know about Paul tells me that he was a strong man of rugged constitution – even before his conversion. I cannot imagine that he easily chose to weakly fall on his knees and **beg**. He was hurting – bad. But God wanted him to be weakened. God used the suffering of this strong man to make him humble enough to choose to depend entirely on the power of God and not his own strength. God brought Paul to the point where his own 'strength' was so weak that he *had* to depend on God's strength. God used his suffering and weakness to conform him to the character of Christ.

Was it worth it to Paul to suffer the torment of the thorn in the flesh? I'll let him speak for himself. "So now I am glad to boast about my weaknesses, so that the power of Christ may work through me. Since I know it is all for Christ's good, I am quite content with my weaknesses and with insults, hardships, persecutions, and calamities. For when I am weak, then I am strong." (2Corinthians 12:9b-10, NLT)

Are we willing to let God break us with the kind of suffering that will conform us to the character of Christ and bring us humbly to receive the strength of God? Would that be enough meaning to make the suffering somehow cease to be suffering? Remember, during that time of suffering – as always – He will provide all the gracious favor we need. I say, "It's worth it."

Preparation for Greater Service

I believe it makes some sense that as we become more and more like Christ – possibly through suffering – God also empowers us to be used more fully for his purposes and his glory. He uses our trials to build our character, to bring us to rely more on Him (2Cor. 1:9), to cause us to seek Him desperately and draw us closer to Him, and to teach us to hear His voice more clearly. Each of those attributes is necessary if we seek to serve the Lord to the fullest of our ability in Christ.

Moses had to flee from Egypt to keep from being executed by Pharaoh after he had killed an Egyptian whom he found beating a Hebrew slave. But during his time of exile, Moses came to know God and was called by God to return to Egypt and demand that Pharoah release the Hebrew slaves. Moses gave God every excuse in the book not to go. But God empowered him every step of the way. One can only imagine how much longer the Jewish people would have remained in bondage had Moses chosen to throw in the towel.

Joseph was thrown into a well and left for dead by his brothers. Lucky for him, a group of Midianites happened by and Joseph's brothers decided that there was no sense in killing their brother now that there was a chance to make some money off of him. His brothers sold him to the Midianites, who, in turn, sold him into the hands of an Egyptian officer. That's a bit of tragedy that most of us never encounter. Sold into slavery by your brothers after they first leave you for dead.

Joseph was 18 years-old at the time. He must have been hurting severely. He had reason to rant, "God, where are you?" He had reason to shake his fist and cry out, "My God, why have you abandoned me?" But during Joseph's time of exile and forced service to Potiphar, God was with him and made him prosper. Joseph endured the betrayal of his brother's and God blessed him in it.

But Joseph's troubles were not over. Potiphar's wife took a liking to him. That might have been a good thing, but she liked him more than a bit too much. As the Bible says, she wanted Joseph to lie with her – and she wasn't just talking about telling an untruth.

I would imagine that, being an 18 year-old man at the time, Joseph was, more than likely, rather tempted to satisfy his natural urges with Mrs. Potiphar. She made the request daily and he had reason to say, "Look, God let my brothers throw me down a well and sell me. I'm here in this foreign place with no way out. Why not have a little fun?" But Joseph, in spite of what he suffered, was still serving the Lord. He told Mrs. Potiphar, "I will not sin against my God."

Mrs. Potiphar was none too happy. She falsely accused Joseph of trying to rape her and he was thrown into prison. However, while he was enduring all that prison life had to offer, God was still with him. And Joseph must have been paying close attention because he learned to hear the voice of God. God gave him the ability to interpret dreams.

After being in prison for a number of years, Joseph had the opportunity to interpret the dream of a former cupbearer of Pharaoh who had lost favor and been thrown into the same prison as Joseph. Joseph told the cupbearer that in three days he would be released from prison and restored to his position in Pharaoh's palace. Joseph, hoping to be released himself, asked the cupbearer to remember him when he returned to Pharaoh's service.

The cupbearer was released – and promptly forgot all about Joseph. It was not until two more years later – when Pharaoh had a dream that nobody was able to interpret – that the cupbearer brought Joseph to Pharoah's attention. Joseph was summoned from prison and he correctly interpreted Pharaoh's dream, thus gaining his release.

Joseph was 18 when his brothers sold him as a slave. He was 30 when he was released from prison. Let's not underestimate what he endured. He went through one severe hardship after another for 12 years. Sold by his brothers, falsely accused of rape, unjustly sent to prison, and forgotten for two years by a man who could have sprung him from jail. Joseph had reason to give up. What reason did he have for hope? What reason did he have to live? What meaning could there be to such a life?

But in the most miserable circumstances of his life, Joseph found a way to go on. How did he do it? I must return to the words of Viktor Frankl:

> "We must never forget that we may also find meaning in life even when confronted with a hopeless situation, when facing a fate that cannot be changed. For what then matters is to bear witness to the uniquely human potential at its best, which is to transform a personal tragedy into a triumph, to turn one's predica-

ment into a human achievement. When we are no longer able to change a situation . . . we are challenged to change ourselves." (Frankl, 1984, p.135)

There was nothing in Joseph's earthly situation that told him that things would ever get any better. There was nothing that said he would be released from prison. No reason to believe that he would ever return to the land of his father, Jacob. And the only sparse evidence of a promise from God was a dream he had 12 years earlier in which the sun and moon and eleven stars bowed down to him. Surely, over the course of 12 miserable years he gravely doubted that dream, if he even remembered it. But, somehow, rather than being destroyed, he managed to actually prosper to whatever level possible while falsely imprisoned in a foreign country to which he had been sold by his very own brothers.

No matter his circumstances, Joseph did his best at whatever lowly, rotten task he may have been assigned. He endured. He suffered well. And the scriptures say, "But while Joseph was there in the prison, the Lord was with him; he showed him kindness and granted him favor in the eyes of the warden. So the warden put Joseph in charge of all those held in the prison, and he was made responsible for all that was done there. The warden paid no attention to anything under Joseph's care, because the Lord was with Joseph and gave him success in whatever he did." (Genesis 39: 20b-23 NIV)

The scriptures say that the Lord was with Joseph when he was a slave in Potiphar's household and throughout all the years that he was in prison. And it appears that in all he suffered, Joseph never forgot the Lord. He refused Mrs. Potiphar, saying that he would not sin against God, and when he interpreted dreams he gave the glory to God, saying, "Do not interpretations belong to God," and "I cannot do it, but God will give Pharaoh the answer he desires."

So, why all the misery, betrayal, and persecution for this Godly man? He was being prepared for greater service. While a slave, Joseph was put in charge of Potiphar's household and everything he owned. While in prison, he was made responsible for everything that was done there. God was molding him for leadership through what he suffered. And Joseph was learning to hear the voice of God, to trust God, and to depend entirely upon Him. Could that have happened without the misery and false persecution? Perhaps. More likely, Joseph would have become proud of what he perceived to be his own achievements.

Joseph was released from prison when he was summoned to interpret a dream that troubled Pharaoh. Because Joseph had learned to hear the voice of God, he was able to tell Pharaoh God's message in the dream: There would be seven years of abundance in Egypt, followed by seven years of famine. And God gave Joseph the plan that would preserve Egypt during the famine.

The 12 years of betrayal and persecution had been used by God to prepare Joseph for this moment. He had been given a small amount of responsibility as a slave to Potiphar and more when he was thrown into a dungeon. Because he had remained faithful to God through what he suffered, Joseph was now prepared to lead the entire nation. He had faced a hopeless situation that he could not change and triumphed by changing himself – through the grace of God. (Frankl, 1984, p.135)

How is God preparing you during your times of trial? What might He have in store? How is he asking you to change? I hope it doesn't take 12 years to get through it, but even if it does, He will provide the grace. Get close to Him in the darkness and you will be ready when He lights up your path.

In the Book of Ecclesiasticus (also known as "Sirach") which is recognized by the Catholic Church, though not Protestants, as canonical, there is the following verse: "My son, if you seek to serve the Lord, prepare yourself for an ordeal. For chosen men are tested in the furnace of humiliation. (Ecclesiasticus 2:1, 5 The Jerusalem Bible)

It would seem to make perfect sense that those who desire to go into full-time ministry should expect to undergo some form of pretty serious trials, insults, weaknesses, hardships and persecutions. Would that not seem to be required preparation for one who hopes to lead others through their own trouble?

There is, thanks to sin entering the scene, much suffering in the world. As ministers, we are called to deal with the deep agony of others – in a way so intimate that it not only touches us, but grabs hold and shakes us until we are transformed. If we want that transformation to be in the direction of Christ, then we need to get to know him in our own deep sorrow and pain. When we find Him there, we will be able to take Him with us into the deep sorrow and pain of those to whom we minister. And they will know not merely that we are with them, but that He is with them in us. Would that give meaning to the suffering we have endured? I think that makes it all more than worth the trouble.

> "My son, if you aspire to serve the Lord,
>   prepare yourself for an ordeal.
> Be sincere of heart, be steadfast,
>   and do not be alarmed when disaster comes.
> Cling to him and do not leave him,
>   so that you may be honored at the end of your days.
> Whatever happens to you, accept it,
>   and in the uncertainties of your humble state, be patient,
> since gold is tested in the fire,
>   and chosen men in the furnace of humiliation.
> Trust him and he will uphold you,
>   follow a straight path and hope in him."
>   (Ecclesiasticus 2: 1-6, The Jerusalem Bible).

Did you notice the words "_furnace of humiliation_?" Once we have come through that, desperately, fearfully clinging to Christ for all He is worth, then we are fully equipped to march into somebody else's furnace.

I am reminded that immediately after Jesus was baptized and immediately before he began his ministry, the Holy Spirit *drove* him into the desert where he remained for forty days and was tempted by satan. (Mark 1:9-13) The *Holy Spirit* 'drove' him there. Talk about being prepared through suffering.

Abraham Biggs, a 19 year-old man who had bipolar disorder and tragically committed suicide, has demanded an answer from me: "How dare you call bipolar a blessing?"

I was two-thirds finished with the writing of this book when I first read of Abraham Biggs, but I know that everything I have here written, both after *and before* hearing of Abraham (the entire book), is in response to his question. Is my answer sufficient. Maybe not. But I will keep on believing that there is blessing in the very act of suffering – even if it never ends this side of home. I must believe it. And I must fight for it.

At this very moment there is another 19 year-old man alone somewhere with a thunderstorm cracking fire through his bipolar brain. He is fighting. And he desperately, ragingly, wants a reason to keep on fighting. He wants a reason to believe that he can "change and improve." That he can love and be love-able and is loveable.

Abraham Biggs is demanding that I let that 19 year old man know that he can be blessed. That he can *be a blessing*. I am called to let that 19-year-old know that there is a reason for him to live. A reason to keep on fighting. A reason that is more profound and noble than anything he could now possibly imagine.

That gives my past sufferings with bipolar all the meaning they need. They have, indeed, somehow ceased to be suffering.

"Out of the bad comes the good."
  - Aloysius Jarnevich

CHAPTER 7

FAITH THAT MAKES WORKS COME ALIVE

Where there is faith, there will be works. Faith will be manifested in the fruit of a believer's life. This does not mean that without works the believer is not saved. Rather that there is a positive change in the believer when he comes to believe. The change (manifested in the life he now lives) does not save him. It demonstrates that he is already saved by faith in the death and resurrection of Christ. However, if there are no works to demonstrate the change, one has to wonder whether there is any faith and, hence, whether the alleged believer really does believe.

Abraham's faith was credited to him as righteousness, but not until he demonstrated that faith by obeying God, tying his only son, Isaac, to the altar of sacrifice, and raising the knife to the boy's throat. He showed God that he was for real. That his faith was genuine. Abraham's faith had changed him into a man who was ready to do whatever God asked or commanded.

The change in me was immediate and permanent– twenty years ago. But it will not be complete until I meet final sanctification upon passing from this earth into real life – when I die and go to heaven.

I have no children- and at 46 that possibility becomes less likely everyday – but I'm fairly certain that if I did marry and my wife did conceive, I would be unwilling to put the child on the altar. Fortunately, I am also certain that God no longer asks us to take such extreme action. (He was doing something unique for all eternity with Abraham.) But He does expect positive changes in me to be manifested everyday - because He planted His Holy Spirit in me to make those changes happen. I cannot do it on my own and God does not ask me to. He remembers that I am dust. (Psalm 103:14)

What is different about me since I became a believer?

What was my "faith" like prior to my 1988 crack-up and hospitalization?

The person I was prior to going into the hospital in 1988 – prior to giving my life to Christ – has never been seen again. He was changed forever and did not emerge from the hospital. That person had been searching for God and seeking to know Him, but not to the point of asking Him for help with his life and emotions, and not to the point of knowing and accepting that Christ's crucifixion was the penalty – paid in full – for his sin.

Catholicism had taught me that "Jesus died for our sins," but my understanding fell short. I understood that because we sin, Jesus went to the Cross. But I did not recognize that I deserve to be nailed to that Cross and that Christ went there *instead* of me.

Faith in Christ and acceptance of His work on the Cross as the payment (penance) for my sin freed me to change mentally, emotionally, and spiritually. The guilt was broken, both in the sense of my record of sin being expunged and in the sense of my being relieved of that fierce and persistent, damning emotion.

Giving up that guilt was, in itself, one of those works that demonstrates faith. It is something that I had not been able to do prior to going into the psych ward, dropping to my knees on the hospital floor, and whispering, "Yes," to everything Christ has done for me. A whisper was all I could manage. And it was all the work God was looking for in that initial moment of my faith. That whisper was the work that manifested my faith. It demonstrated an emotional change in me that was only possibly by grace through faith in Christ.

Yes, faith without works is dead, but there is "work" in the very act of coming to genuine faith in Christ. As Jesus said, "This is the work of God, that you believe in the One He sent." (John 6:29 New American Bible).

Prior to going into the hospital my faith was dead, as in lifeless. Whatever the nature of my 'belief' in a god at that time, it made little difference in the way I was living my life or the way I viewed myself and the world – except, possibly, to make me angry with myself for not living up to some vague and ever-changing standard.

My vague beliefs before coming to faith in Christ were no more than a mental groping for the truth whether it led to Christ, some god of my own creation, self-actualization (whatever that is), or no god at all. Openness to the probability of God is about as far as I went in May 1988, in spite of my commitment to Christ at my confirmation in the Catholic church 12 years earlier at the age of 14. Was I saved? God knows. But I am glad that I wasn't taken off this earth – and didn't take myself off of it – prior to falling on my knees in St. Francis hospital in July 1988.

A desire for God is a yearning in the right direction, but without surrender to Christ it does not bring salvation. It is not faith. A mere desire for God does not transform one's essence, one's core, one's eternal identity and destiny. It is not accompanied by the works that faith manifests.

I had an openness to the probability of God – and even a desire for the possibility of Christ – long before I first heard behind me the locking of the psych ward doors. And God, thank God, used that to drag and pull my stubborn hide through hell to Him.

It was the stubbornness that made the hell necessary. If I had been humble and wise enough to truly surrender to the King of kings short of hell, I could have avoided it altogether. For some us things have to get fiery bad. But God was faithful. He wanted me so badly that He was willing to let me choose to go through hell in order to be convinced not only that

He is real, but that I desperately need Him. That I have <u>*never*</u> survived one moment without Him.

Going through the hell of depression was NOT a work that demonstrated my faith. The demonstration, however, did come in the despairing depths of that hell when I finally gave up my pride. The pride that said, "I have to make it on my own – without God, without Christ, without a Savior dying on the Cross the death that I deserve." That pride nearly killed me and giving it up was hard work. But was it my work or God's? I don't know. I do believe, however, that without the pain, guilt, introversion, extroversion, energy, and glimpses of unbridled joy that come with bipolar disorder, I may not have recognized my sin and my need for Christ. I may have just been blissfully ignorant of my impending doom if I had not been blessed with a small taste of it here on earth. Praise God, I am bipolar! Hallelujah!

CHAPTER 8

NOTES FROM THE NUTHOUSE

During a recent review of a couple of old notebooks, I stumbled upon some pages I wrote while I was hospitalized at Western Psychiatric Institute and Clinic in the summer of 2006. I will present them here, only slightly edited from the psych ward version, as evidence that even in severe moods the bipolar brain can produce at least moderately clear thinking. (Maybe not. You be the judge.) But allow me to first provide some brief background on the events that led to my voluntary admission to the hospital.

I had learned that the cataracts on both of my eyes may have been caused by the seroquel my psychiatrist had prescribed to treat bipolar. I handled that news alright for about two days. I kept a lid on my anger and told myself that the surgery on my left eye would be a blessing that would give me better vision than I had before the cataract developed. I could tell myself that for only so long. The cataract-seroquel connection gnawed at me – silently at first. Then it started to grab hold and speak. "You should have been told that this could happen. You could have refused the (<u>curse</u>) medication. You were taking too much anyway. It knocked you out." By day three I was speaking it out loud – cursing, yelling, stomping around the house, ready to tear into my doctor and the hospital, and cranking up a medical malpractice case on the strength of my expulsion lawsuit.

I stormed into the Western Psych emergency room, demanding a change in medication, treatment for my bleary cloud-coated eyes, and tests of my blood sugar levels (another potential side effect of seroquel). I was so enraged that the young doctor who interviewed me admitted bravely, "You're starting to scare me."

I glared. My voice went deep, slow, and red-hot bold. "It is my . . . <u>Intention</u> . . . to scare you!"

"It's working."

"My doctor!" I growled lowly, "who works for this hospital, gave . . . me . . . cataracts! And this hospital is going to do something about it . . . Now." I went on in low-growl. "I am going to be admitted and I am going to be treated. This place is going to take care of my eyes, test my blood sugar, and change my medication." My teeth clenched and I stared from the back of my head through the wall behind the doctor.

"Oh . . . uh, you'll be admitted," he rushed, standing his ground as though ducking a blow. "That's no problem."

"Good. This needs to get done."

My father and mother visited me daily while I was in the hospital. My dad visited twice a day, once in the afternoon while my mom was at work and then later with her. He brought me lunch, a broccoli-cheese-bacon casserole type of gruel that I can't get enough of.

My parents had planned to visit my sisters in Tennessee. I assured them that they should go regardless of my being in the hospital. In fact, I would have felt awful if they had missed the trip because of me. Before they left my dad brought me a 9-and-three-quarter inch by 7-and-a-half inch black 100 sheet Composition Book. On the cover he printed my name and the phone numbers of my brother Pete and my sister Judy who both live near us in Pittsburgh.

Eventually, I settled down and began the following psych ward scribblings:

Anger Management

Anger is not just the result of an event that happens in my life or something somebody says or does. It also involves my thoughts about those events and the things people say or do. I can change my thinking (self-talk) so that I won't get angry or will be able to deal effectively with my anger.

For example, if I don't get a job I want, instead of saying, "I'm a failure," I can say, "I tried my best. I was qualified for the job, but for some reason that has nothing to do with me they hired somebody else.

It was good practice at interviewing and will help me get an even better job."

I can notice signs that I am getting angry:

- *muscles tighten, get tense*
- *chest tightens*
- *breathing becomes quicker*
- *my face feels warm, flushed*

And then remove myself from the situation until I can appropriately deal with it.

Use Slogan:

"I will not let this get the best of me."

Pray:

"Holy Spirit, stabilize my emotions in the righteousness of Christ."

"God, make me quick to listen, slow to speak, and slow to get angry."

I am not a failure. I have had the courage to try a number of things and have often succeeded.

- *I have tried many jobs*
- *I have run a marathon*
- *I have a masters degree*
- *I went to law school on a full-tuition, merit-based scholarship*

- *I am effectively trying a complex lawsuit prose*
- *I have filed an appeal with the 11th Circuit Federal Court of Appeals*
- *I have successfully counseled many people*
- *I work-out 5 days per week*
- *I weigh the same as I did when I was 16 years old*
- *I am an excellent communicator*
- *I am able to discuss my feelings*
- *I can sing well*
- *I stood up for a family in court when the county tried to take their kids. I testified for them against the county agency that funded my program. Judge agreed with me.*
- *Nobody at Club Julian can come close to my performance on the versaclimber, stepmill, or Jacob's Ladder.*
- *I earned football scholarships to Georgia Tech, Louisville, William and Mary, and Northeastern.*
- *I stood up for Amanda against her school district and convinced them to put her in a special education program (and treat agoraphobia)rather than expelling her (for chronic truancy). District's School Psychologist agreed with me.*

(Sitting here looking at all of this two years later the thought strikes me, "Man, God has really blessed you! How in the world did you get so depressed that you landed in the psych ward?" But that was the idea. I wrote these statements about my successes <u>while</u> I was in the hospital as a method for trying to work myself out of depression and find ways to avoid it in the future.)

<u>Don't jump to conclusions</u> about events, or things people say or do, that could make you angry. Get all the facts. <u>Assume the most benign explanation</u>.

Christian Affirmations

"I can do all things through Christ who strengthens me."

"I am a saint, filled with the Holy Spirit and today I will walk in the power of the Holy Spirit."

"I know that in <u>All Things</u> God is working for my good."

"THE SAME HOLY SPIRIT WHO RAISED CHRIST FROM THE DEAD IS THE HOLY SPIRIT WHO LIVES IN ME!"

"God created me just a little lower than the angels."

"I have been in the furnace of humiliation because I <u>am</u> God's chosen man!"

"The Sovereign, Omnipotent, Creator-King of the universe is my Dad and He loves me more than I can possibly imagine."

Proverbs 12:24 "work hard and become a leader; Be lazy and become a slave."

Exodus 15:3 "The Lord is a warrior; yes, the Lord is His name!"

"God will not let me suffer death until I have fulfilled the mission He has for me."

"In Christ I am more than a conqueror."

(I, right now, feel strengthened just typing these affirmations. I can feel the power of the Holy Spirit rising up in me. I just noticed that my fists are clenched, not in anger, but in the power of the Holy Spirit. You must try roaring these affirmations out loud when you are down in the dumps. Stand up, yell, and throw your fists in the air! Believe these affirmations as you say them and there will be change. You will enter the Presence of God. I dare ya.)

"Greater is He who is in me than he who is in the world."

"God is preparing me for something greater, something wonderful, the ministry/mission to which He is calling me."

"Chosen men are tested in the furnace of humiliation."

"God is preparing me and sending me to fight to win justice for the oppressed. And I will not only be fighting to win justice, I will be fighting to win souls!"

There is a pattern to my depression and anger that I must break. First, I do now realize that not everything that could make me depressed or angry does make me angry. There are times when I react to provocation and frustration calmly and without depression.
Pattern

1. *Frustrating event*
2. *I interpret the event as a problem*
3. *I continue to tell myself that the event is a problem*
4. *I tell myself that the event is a major problem without knowing whether it actually is a problem.*
5. *I begin to think about event obsessively*
6. *I become depressed*
7. *I tell myself that everything, or many things, in my life are a major problem or that they are broken.*
8. *I feel hopeless*
9. *I become angry*
10. *I manifest anger by yelling, cursing, stomping through the house.*

I CAN BREAK THIS PATTERN BY INJECTING A POSITIVE THOUGHT OR BEHAVIOR WHICH IS CONTRARY TO THE PATTERN AT ANY STAGE OF THE PROCESS.

- *Christian affirmations*
- *List of accomplishments*
- *List of abilities*
- *Miracles God has done in my life*

STRATEGY FOR COPING

1. *Recognize that I may not know all the facts about the frustrating event.*
2. *Tell myself that it may not be a problem. There may be a benign explanation.*
3. *If the event is a problem, do not overestimate the size of it. "Tell your problem how big your God is." (Jeff Leake, Senior Pastor, Allison Park Church of the Assemblies of God).*
4. *Use Christian Affirmations*
5. *Slogan: I will not let this get the best of me.*
6. *Reject negative self-talk*
7. *Recognize obsessive thinking and counter it with positive self-talk*
8. *Recognize that I have overcome many problems*
9. *Don't jump to conclusions*
10. *Call Gerry* (my counselor) *or Dr. Mullick*

POSITIVE SELF-TALK

- *In the hospital they called me "superman"*
- *Mrs. Jacobs said she thought that I was about 32 years old when I was actually 44.*
- *A person I admire once called me "a beautiful Christian man."*
- *Judy, my sister, said that she never thought that my ears were big.*
- *I am made in the image and likeness of God*
- *I am being conformed to the character of Christ*
- *I am the champion* (at Club Julian) *on the versaclimber, stepmill, and Jacob's Ladder*

3/21/06
How depression/anger/mixed mania feels.
I am writing this as an in-patient at WPIC. I was admitted on 3/16/06.

It's like a thunderstorm in my brain. There is pain and pressure and heaviness inside my head, a dull aching. Everything is darkness. Every sound is a crashing noise. I am hopeless, angry, depressed and feeling like there is no way out, no future, no way to change my life. The past is filled with error and failure. The present is agony. And there is no future.

When I felt like this I was taking 50mg. of Zoloft, 1500 mg. of depakote, and 200mg. of seroquel.

I feel much better now. There is no pain or pressure in my head. My mind is clear. There is no heaviness or dull aching. I can function. I believe I can get a good job. I smile. I talk with people. I laugh. I'm interested again in the things I used to be interested in – people, the Pirates, working-out (I exercised daily in my hospital room. That's why they called me superman.), *the Bible, prayer.*

I'm not dwelling on broken relationships and my expulsion and lawsuit.

I feel more alert, cheerful, and energized than I have in weeks. I got out of bed and started moving more quickly than I have in a long time.

*I MUST REMEMBER, I MUST ADMIT, THAT THE IMPROVEMENT IN MY MOOD WAS CAUSED BY THE **INCREASE** IN MY MEDS. Remember this when you are tempted to take less medication. Taking less w/o Dr.'s approval will cause me to be angry, hopeless, and depressed – AGONY.*

*Report side effects to Doctor, but do **NOT** decrease dosage on your own. Sooner or later it will cause deep agony, an anguish that you believe will last forever. Decreasing meds. will cause your thinking to become distorted.*

This has happened too many times not to admit it and accept it.

I am now taking 100 mg Zoloft, 2000 mg. depakote, and 400 mg seroquel.

Shortly after being discharged from the psych ward, I gave the above notes to my outpatient counselor, Gerry Price. He read them and made a copy which he keeps in my file. If I go excessively bipolar for any extended period (even my now normal moods are still, and will always be, more intense than those of a person who does not have bipolar – and I like it that way), my counselor has my permission to challenge me with my own words. That ought to be enough to bring me to my senses and back into treatment.

As I was discharged from the hospital, the social worker scheduled me to see Gerry a couple of days later. After meeting with him for that counseling session on April 5, 2006, I wrote the following:

> *I saw Gerry Price today for a counseling appointment. He made a lot of sense. I told him about what I have written in this notebook about my anger management plan, the pattern of my anger and depression, and my commitment to taking the exact amount of meds prescribed. He said that I had good insight.*
>
> *Gerry has counseled about 150 people with bipolar disorder; some of whom are doctors, judges, lawyers, and nurses. He gave me his card and encouraged me to call and leave a message if I am having trouble. His phone is off during the day. If it is an emergency, I can call the receptionist and she will contact him. If I need to talk with somebody in the evening or on the weekend, I can call the Diagnostic and Evaluation Center. They have mobile crisis teams available.*

I had been treated for depression and bipolar disorder since 1988 and had been continuously in treatment since 1994, but this was the first time I had truly committed to using any and all of the resources available to me that I may need. I firmly decided that

I would no longer put my family through the hell of being my first line of defense against my most severe symptoms. Since that time I have called Gerry on the few occasions when I have felt like I was about to explode. He called back quickly and the meltdown was averted. I have missed one or two counseling appointments when I was out of town, but I quickly called and scheduled another appointment. It works. And I will do and use whatever is necessary to keep me from going over the edge.

*"You can stand me up at the gates of hell,
but I'll stand my ground.
And I won't back down."*
- Tom Petty (1989)

CHAPTER 9

DELUSIONS OF GRANDEUR

If you could pick which mental illness you would like to have, bipolar disorder would be the only sane choice. What other "illness," mental or physical, has documented clinical symptoms like elation, unbridled energy, and delusions of grandeur?

Don't get me wrong. All of the above, when taken to extremes, can cause some real trouble. There are those, who, in the height of mania, spend all of their money and their life-savings, max out all of their credit cards, and bet the mortgage on a not-so-sure thing. There are also people who go on sexual rampages during the wild energy and elation of a manic episode. Both the spending and sex sprees – as wondrous as they may seem – will destroy you.

When you are wired out-of-control with energy, not needing any sleep, and sky-high with plans beyond anyone's capacity; it is not time to jump into bed with anyone and everyone who is willing and/or spend a second mortgage on a can't miss proposition. IT IS TIME TO GET TO THE EMERGENCY ROOM. (Remember, this is coming from somebody who was once so angry about being in a psych ward that he kicked open a dead-bolted metal door and made a run for it.) I do not like being an inpatient in a mental hospital, but it beats ending up as a bankrupt, single parent with AIDS because you didn't get treatment for your out-of-control manic elation, energy, and delusions of grandeur. GET TO THE EMERGENCY ROOM!

Okay, now that I have stated that warning, I want to let you know that manic elation, energy, and delusions of grandeur, when gently but securely harnessed, can be productive – and a whole lot of fun.

When I am in that hypomanic zone, I get all kinds of ideas about what I might like to do and who I might want to be. I dream. I imagine myself taking action toward some lofty mad project. I make plans – big plans – unfettered by thoughts of failure or the paralyzing drain of being unrealistic. I think new thoughts about old perspectives. I have the energy to get things done and I believe that I can do them. Once, I even had the grand delusion that I could write a book.

Sure, most of my "delusions" do not work out. The vast majority of them never get off the ground. And some of them, indeed, must never be attempted. But that hypomanic brainstorm is a soaring wonder that I refuse to allow my medication to take away from me. (*I do take the medication, I just don't let it rob me.*) It changes the way I look at the world. It makes me see beautiful possibilities that are completely unrealistic until somebody tries to accomplish them. It motivates me to look silly going passionately after greater things – like a real relationship with a living God. Any good thing I have ever accomplished started out in my imagination. So, why not let it run bipolar wild?

If I did not first dream it, I never would have earned a football scholarship. I would not have a masters degree in psychology. I never would have run a full mile, much less the 1997 Pittsburgh Marathon. And I would not have gone to law school or sued a university pro se in federal court.

In addition to empowering me to see possibilities, make plans, set goals, and take action, my mildly controlled "delusions" can make life a little more playful and interesting. And since I hate boredom and love solitude, getting "grandiose" (St. Thomas University's psychologist's description of me) can come in handy when I need to amuse and entertain my own bipolar brain. And I can do it in the privacy of my own mystic contemplation, whenever I want and regardless of my circumstances – sort of like prayer.

One of the delusions in which I choose to engage almost daily has me functioning as the general manager of the Pittsburgh Pirates, my favorite professional sports team. They have not had a winning season in sixteen years. I love taking on the challenge of turning that operation around. Anybody could build a winner with the Yankees payroll. I'm bipolar. I dream big. I want to win with one-quarter of that money.

Over the years of my term as GM, I have drafted college players, signed mid-level free agents, made waiver claims, and negotiated numerous trades. I have projected rosters, batting orders, and starting pitching rotations years in advance. Getting this team to contend is a big job and to most "fans" it seems an impossible quest. But somebody's got to do it. And I'm at work.

Hey, it keeps me from depression and the semi-friendly confines of the psych ward. And it's not as though I'm marching into the clubhouse and sending players to Triple A Indianapolis or the Altoona Curve. However, I do bear a slight resemblance to Billy Beane, GM of the Oakland A's. And it could be fun to pass myself off as him at the next winter meetings.

Another hypomanic flight of fancy that has at times occupied my bipolar-ness is that of being a traveling preacher. One might say that there is nothing so "grandiose" about that vision. There are many ministers who, rather than being employed at one specific church, travel to various churches throughout a region of the country to preach and conduct seminars for a weekend or several days. But, lest ye forget, I have bipolar disorder and, therefore, my "vision" must go stratospheric. I fantasize about walking from church to church across the whole country, preaching, counseling, and evangelizing at every random opportunity along the road.

What a way to witness! Every time somebody unwittingly asks, "How ya doin," I can respond, "I'm walkin' across the country, preachin' the gospel."

Imagine this:

A twenty-year-old female clerk in a 7-Eleven greets a sun-burnt, bright-eyed, and hungry me with some variation of "What's up?"

"O-o-o-h, just walkin' cross the country preachin' the gospel," I beam wistfully like a nut.

"Oh . . . um, wha'did you say?"

"I'm walkin' across the whole U.S. of A., going from church to church talking to people about Jesus."

She laughs. "You're not serious," she says, almost considering the possibility.

"Serious? Heck, no," I reply, "I'm blessed."

She gives me that familiar "What-a-goofy-ass" look – curled lip, half-squint, raised brow, grinning part-smirk. "Yeah," she says, "I'm not quite sure I'd wanna be blessed like that."

And I launch. "I can't help it. There is nothing in my life more important than Jesus Christ. So, I studied, took some ministry courses, and started walking. I'm just tryin' to pass on this incredible gift God gave me. It's amazing. Gets better all the time. And everybody can have it – free – forever."

"I'm sure I'd love to hear about it, pal, but I got customers behind ya."

"Oh, yeah. Well, go ahead," I say, "Take care of 'em. I can wait."

And by the pure grace of God, the skinny old man behind me with the three-day growth, sunglasses, dirty old baseball cap, and dip between his cheek and gum says, "Go ahead, son, tell her 'bout that gift God give us."

I'll tell ya, sometimes, I can't think of a better way to live out the rest of my days. Of course, there is that general manager of the Pirates delusion. You see, first, we change the name of the team to the Preaching Pirates or Pirate-Pastors (stealing souls for Christ). And, instead of the Star Spangled Banner, we sing God Bless America. No, The Battle Hymn of the Republic.

Can't you hear it? Just before the game starts. "Glory, glory, hallelujah. Glory, glory hallelujah. Glory, glory hallelujah. His truth is marching on!" How could we possibly lose after that?

Yes! Yes! Yes! Marching across the country, heart-ablaze, preaching the gospel in the off-season between the close of the World Series and the start of spring training. Now, why would any psychiatrist want to rob me of that joyful delusion?

Here's another:

On May 15, 2007, Primary Election Day in Pennsylvania, I wrote in my own name for three different Judge positions – Common Pleas Court of Allegheny County, Pennsylvania Superior Court, and Pennsylvania Supreme Court – and Allegheny County Chief Executive.

No, I did not win and I held no illusions about the possibility. But, hey, I didn't like any of the candidates and writing myself in seemed like the bipolar thing to do. I meet the constitutional requirements. I am a U.S. citizen and a resident of Allegheny County in the Commonwealth of Pennsylvania. At 45, I surely meet the age requirement. And nobody can accuse me of apathy – I did vote.

Do you really think that I would be the first bipolar judge to take the bench in Pennsylvania?

On the other hand, I don't know of any judges who were elected after having been expelled from law school. Maybe I'll organize a write-in campaign under the biblical banner: One can indeed come out of prison to reign. (Ecclesiastes 4:14a)

And, now, yet another of my harmless jaunts into bipolar grandeur:

On July 1, 2008, I imagined myself as a speech writer for Senator John McCain during his 2008 Presidential campaign. Two days earlier, retired General Wesley Clark, a former candidate for the 2004 democratic presidential nomination, had said that Senator McCain's heroism as a prisoner of war for five years during the Vietnam War did not qualify him to be President of the United States. General Clark also said that McCain was 'isolated" during the Vietnam War and did not have any executive experience in the military.

I was bothered by the General's comments, but even more so by the Senator's lack of a vigorous response. Therefore, in a mildly symptomatic "delusion," I dreamed up the following speech for Senator McCain to hypothetically deliver.

"General Wesley Clark has said that my experience as a prisoner of war for five years in North Vietnam does not qualify me to be President of the United States. The General is correct. I was a P.O.W. for five years, but I was not alone. Many brave American soldiers were tortured by that brutal enemy of the United States. However, General Clark is correct. That experience, simply doing my duty for my country, does not, in itself, qualify me to be President.

"But I do believe those years say something about my willingness to pay the price of my citizenship. Those five years in a Vietnamese prison camp say something about my willingness to stand up for my country – no matter what the cost!

"And, General Clark, it also says something about a man's willingness to stand up for his country when he spends twenty years in the church of a pastor who prays for God to damn America. It says something about a man's willingness to stand up for his country when he stays in the church of a pastor who, on September 16, 2001, five days after 9/11, called the terrorist attacks on the Pentagon and the World Trade Center Towers 'America's chickens coming home to roost.'

For nearly seven years after Jeremiah Wright said that America got what it deserved on 9/11, Barack Obama stayed in Pastor Wright's church. For nearly seven years, Barack Obama continued to financially support Jeremiah Wright <u>after</u> Wright preached that *the murder of 3,000 innocent U.S. citizens was just America getting what it had coming to it. Barack Obama stayed in that church for seven more years.*

"Barack Obama did not stand up to his pastor and defend his country. No, he continued to call that anti-American pastor his spiritual advisor and mentor. That, General Clarke, says something about Senator Obama's willingness to stand up for his country. That, General Clarke, says something about Senator Obama's willingness to pay the price of his citizenship.

"Senator Obama supported his anti-American pastor with tens of thousands of dollars over twenty years. Yes, General Clarke, that does say something about Senator Obama's qualifications to lead this country.

"And, now, Senator Obama promises to sit down with the leader of Iran and talk with that sponsor of terrorism – without pre-conditions. Let me ask you. If Senator Obama cannot stand up to his own anti-American mentor, how in the world can we expect him to stand up to Ahmadinejad?! In fact, given Mr. Obama's allegiance to Reverend Wright, I have to wonder whether he wants to stand up to Ahmadinejad. Perhaps, he just wants to sit down for a cup of herbal tea, talk things over, and maybe apologize for whatever it was that made the terrorists bring the 'chickens home to roost on 9/11.'

General Clarke is correct when he says that five years in a North Vietnamese prison camp does not qualify me to be President. But General Clarke fails to mention that while we were in those prison camps, *there were people in this country who <u>violently</u> protested against us, the American soldiers fighting that war. One of the leaders of those <u>violent</u> and unlawful protests was William Ayers, a man whom Barack Obama now calls his friend.*

"William Ayers, an alleged American citizen, bombed the Pentagon and the Capitol building. He said he was protesting the Vietnam War. I was told about those bombings by North Vietnamese prison guards. Enemy prison guards who hoped that Ayers' bombings would break my will.

"William Ayers – on September 11, 2001 – said that he did not regret bombing the Pentagon and Capitol. He said that he wished that he had done more. Barack Obama calls this man his friend. Barack Obama sits on a board of directors with this man, William Ayers. I was in a Vietnamese prison camp when William Ayers bombed those buildings.

"No, General Clarke, my time in North Vietnam does not qualify me to be President. But it does say something about my undying love for this country. It does say something about my patriotism. Just as Barack Obama's twenty year allegiance to Jeremiah Wright and his friendship with the terrorist, William Ayers, tells us something about Senator Obama's patriotism.

"Patriotism! The American people should not have to question the patriotism of a man running for President of the United States of America. The American people must know – must KNOW – that their President is a patriot. And they must know that

their President will be no friend of terrorists – foreign or domestic.

"Yes. Yes. Yes! God <u>bless</u> America!"

That speech may sound a little rough, but a Christian man is not called to be a wimp. A Christian man is called to tell the truth and take a stand for what is right. And, sometimes, it just might take a bipolar Christian man to get it done.

It obviously goes without saying that I voted for John McCain for President in November 2008. I preferred Mitt Romney (yes, the Mormon candidate whose personal values and governmental principles align well with mine) or Fred Thompson, but they were not on the ballot in November. I wanted John McCain to win the general election. He didn't. And, now, I pray that Barack Obama will be the best President this country has ever known.

So, what value was there in writing the speech if I knew that it was nothing more than my own fantasy? It got the frustration off of my chest and, more importantly, out of my mind. And the grand bipolar delusion of writing that speech allows me the comforting delusion that my speech could have turned the election. (Hey, it's not like I went to a campaign event, barged my way up to the podium, and commanded Senator McCain to give my speech. That would be insane.)

I want to close this chapter by reiterating that delusions of grandeur can be a dangerous and destructive symptom of bipolar disorder. When one does not recognize them as grandiose, they can lead to wildly unrealistic expectations of self and others, bizarre and threatening actions taken in the belief that one has already accomplished the delusion, broken relationships, and a crash of disappointment that will lead to excruciating depression. However, I hope that I have also demonstrated that, when gently but securely harnessed and recognized as imagination, this symptom can be productive – and a whole lot of fun.

"Early Illusions"

Early illusions are beautiful,
Early illusions are wounding.
But what does it matter! We are above
 vanity,
We embrace the highest knowledge,
saved by our happy blindness.

We, who are not afraid of taking a false step –
Fools, from the common point of view—
Still keep enchantment in our faces
Through all the disillusioned crowd.

We are driven towards the distance
 by a glimmering of something,
away from the daily grind, the calculations
 of everyday living,
from pale skeptics and pink schemers,
transforming the world with our reflections.

But the inevitability of disappointments
makes us see too clearly . . . On all sides
everything suddenly takes shape,
all unknown to us till now.

The world appears before us, unhazed;
  unmisted;
no longer radiant with something priceless,
but with all this truthfulness unmasked
as deceit. But what is gone—
  was no deception.

You see, it is not the knowledge of the
  serpent,
it is not the doubtful honor of experience,
but the ability to be enchanted by the world
that reveals to us the world as it really is.

Suppose someone with illusions in his eyes
flashes past, pursuing some distant gleam,
then it doesn't seem to us that he is blind—
it seems to us that we ourselves are blind.

Yevtushenko (1967)
(in <u>Murray</u>, 1986, p.256)

CHAPTER 10

"... A METHOD WHICH REPEATEDLY FAILS MAY POSSIBLY BE WRONG."

—⚋—

I cannot take credit for the title of this section, but, through stubborn trial and damnable error, I have found it to be true. I read it in an article entitled "Republicans and Blacks." (Sowell, realclearpolitcs.com, April 10, 2008) It was written by Thomas Sowell, a 78 year-old black man who is an economist and author of a number of books on topics ranging from basic economics to education to race and social policy.

(I only mention Mr. Sowell's race because of the title of his article in which he addresses ways in which the republican party can successfully appeal to black voters.)

I find Mr. Sowell to be brilliant and would read anything he has authored regardless of subject and without any recommendation further than the by-line featuring his name, but even he attributed the above quote to an anonymous "someone."

Though it is profoundly obvious that a method which repeatedly fails may possibly be wrong, it has been every bit as profoundly difficult for my bipolar brain to process that axiom. I have in the past – let's hope permanently past – repeatedly employed continuously failing methods.

With regard to bipolar disorder, I have often felt that I could and should overcome it on my own. From 1988 through 1994 that theory crashed time and again, yet for six years I refused to see that leaving counseling and giving up on medication was a wrong method.

I was hospitalized four times before I committed to staying on medication for the rest of my life. It is hard for me to imagine that four bipolar episodes serious enough to have landed me in the hospital were not enough to convince me that my ways would not work. What was I thinking? Just try harder? That was a disaster. Every time my mood swung and my mind raced and I screwed something up, I blamed myself for the misfiring of chemicals in my brain. I blamed myself for something over which I had no control rather than taking the medication that could give me some control. A repeatedly failed method.

So what made me finally see that refusing medication was a wrong method? During my fourth hospitalization, I was started – again – on Zoloft. There was no denying that it had an almost immediate impact. Before driving to the hospital I was stomping with depression, agitation, and the distorted logic that told me life could not ever be anything but miserable. It's the kind of mood and thinking that can drive an alienated person needlessly to suicide. Within 48 hours of starting Zoloft, I was feeling good enough to leave the hospital. It was clear that my brain was deficient at maintaining the appropriate levels of serotonin in all the right dark corners. And no amount of my effort, conviction, discipline, pride, and/or perseverance was going to produce more serotonin or keep it where it belongs.

Zoloft is a 'serotonin re-uptake inhibitor.' Zoloft makes serotonin behave. I can't. My brain won't do it. I NEED ZOLOFT. And since this method has not repeatedly failed . . .

It took eleven more years for me to see that not being in a long-term counseling relationship was a wrong method. And counseling has been so wonderfully beneficial that I have no interest in quitting. I want to have the support of a professional available to me – somebody who knows my history, personality, theories about life, and my own unique experience of bipolar disorder. In fact, I may want to have a regular counseling appointment every few weeks for the rest of my life – even if I never have another bipolar episode. My counselor – Gerry Price (UPMC Western Psychiatric) - is an invaluable support. Far better than my failed method of relying on myself and yelling at my parents. It's too bad that I had to fail so many times before I could admit that my method was wrong. My pride caused a lot of pain.

My pride has also insisted that I can overcome sin on my own. Wrong method, brothers and sisters. Perseverance, discipline, commitment, and self-flagellation will not get it done. The enemy will play hell with that brand of pride.

The only method for overcoming sin is surrender. ["There's no success like failure . . ." (Bob Dylan, 1965)] We must admit that we are powerless over sin if we are ever to overcome it. We must give ourselves up to Christ who long ago defeated sin once and forever – for all who surrender to Him.

When I try to battle sin on my own – even as a believer – satan uses my tenacious efforts to condemn me. He tells me that I am no good, none, not in the least part. He tells me that I have failed God and that I am doomed to always fail Him. He beats me up and then he accuses God of injustice. He says, "This God of yours just ain't fair with you. He sees how hard you're trying and He is never satisfied. He'll never be pleased no matter how much you do for Him." And that condemnation and guilt leads me right back into the sin that I felt so damned and guilty for in the first place.

The Apostle Paul was no stranger to this phenomenon. After his conversion, as a passionate believer in Christ, he wrote of himself: "[T]he very commandment that was intended to bring life actually brought death . . . We know that the law is spiritual; but I am unspiritual, sold as a slave to sin. I do not understand what I do. For what I want to do I do not do, but what I hate I do. . . For I have the desire to do what is good, but I cannot carry it out. For what I do is not the good

I want to do; no, the evil I do not want to do – this I keep doing. . . So I find this law at work: When I want to do good, evil is right there with me. . . What a wretched man that I am! . . ." (Romans 7:10,14-15,18b-19, 24a) This was Paul *after* his conversion and *after* he had mightily preached the gospel. He was still tormented by his own sin.

The devil will take my sin and make me feel like a wretched man. The Holy Spirit will take hold of me, call my sin for what it is, and firmly speak, "Richie, you're still my boy. Now, get away from this garbage before it poisons you. Turn back to Christ. Repent. Take hold of what is yours. Be forgiven. Be loved. Now!"

Or as Paul so perfectly put it: "What a wretched man I am! Who will rescue me from this body of death? Thanks be to God – through Jesus Christ our Lord! . . . Therefore, there is now no condemnation for those who are in Christ Jesus, because through Christ Jesus the law of the Spirit of life set me free from the law of sin and death." (Romans 7:24-25, 8:1-2)

Can't you just see Paul jumping for joy with this revelation. He and you and I are now free to stop condemning ourselves. Hallelujah!

We cannot, in and of ourselves, overcome sin. Jesus defeated sin and it must surrender to Him just as a vanquished army must surrender to its victorious foe. But our sin cannot be surrendered to Christ until we are, until we take it to Him to claim the victory we have already won.

If you want to fight sin, dwell with the Holy Spirit. If you want to fight sin, confess it to Christ and receive forgiveness. If you want to fight sin, praise God crazy hard, rejoicing. In any order you choose. And drop that damnable condemnation – it fails every time.

CHAPTER 11

MESSING UP EVERYTHING

I make mistakes constantly. I am absent-minded and I forget things.

Last week I left a hose running in the basement for seven hours.

A month ago, I took my eyes off of the road for a second to change the radio station at the precise moment that the driver in front of me decided to stop her van. I jumped on the brakes of the 1992 Honda Del Sol, swerved to the right, and missed the van. I did, however, run smack into a wooden fence at the edge of somebody's front yard. By the grace of God there was no damage done to the Del Sol – or me – and the repairs to the fence only cost me $70. The owner of the home did me the kindness of putting it back together himself. He was pleased that I did not run off after desecrating his front yard. I pass that place nearly everyday. The Holy Spirit would have banged on me every time.

The fence-crashing is a fairly extreme example, but it makes the point that I am continuously making mistakes. Just yesterday I spilled a cup of coffee on my mother's seven-month old white living room carpet. I cannot think of any mistake I have made this morning, but the day is young.

I do not believe that my error-prone, absent-minded nature has anything to do with bipolar disorder. I chalk it up mostly to being man not God.

The blessing of the error-prone nature is that I have learned and accepted that there isn't much that I can do about it. I am going to mess-up in everything to some degree. The even greater blessing is that accepting the inevitability of messing-up has freed me to try. I don't _ever_ have to be perfect.

[Oh, yeah, I did make a mistake this morning, When I noticed that I am five pounds heavier than I was two months ago, I let myself get upset about it. What non-sense. Five pounds out of 217 on a 6 foot 4 inch frame is imperceptible. It has not slowed me down. And, since it is not a health hazard, I would be a fool to worry myself sick about it.]

There was a time – not so long ago – when my mistakes made me angry. The sin of pride – again. And that often kept me from trying new things. I could not try to learn to play the guitar because I was certain to make mistakes – and the infallible Ya'Zhynka just could not have that. So, in my 46 years, I have never really learned to play the guitar. I have learned to strum a few chords, but putting them together in some melodic rhythm has yet escaped me. You would not want to hear it.

Let me give an example of how knowing that I will screw-up has helped me to succeed.

I heard a man today say that a public speaking class caused him great anxiety. Every time he had to get up and say something he felt his face flush, his heart pounded, and sweat formed in places seen and unseen.

Public speaking does not cause me any concern. I do not expect or hope that every word will be perfect. I expect to occasionally pause too long, forget some ideas and phrases, stutter a few times, not be completely understood, and have some people forever disagree with what I am saying. And I don't care.

Knowing all of this beforehand takes away the anxiety. I can just get up and let it rip without having every word carefully scripted. Let's face it, I would not write a perfect script, either. And isn't it deadly boring when somebody _reads_ a prepared statement, rather blasting away with a 'let-it-rip' speech – with all its errors, emotions, hesitations, stutters, and quirky improvisations? It is a thing of wonder to see a speechmaker get struck with some new insight right in the middle of speaking and go mad with it, glancing around, near-puzzled, searching for the words to express this lightning bolt that he is not quite sure of.

Yes. Yes. Yes! I want to hear sermons like that. I want to _give_ sermons like that. The Holy Spirit striking right in the midst of it, "Hang on there, friend, how's about some fresh revelation right here and now?!" Might take some nerve to risk that kind of mistake, now, wouldn't it? Might even take some bipolar nerve.

CHAPTER 12

MEDS vs. BOOZE

I was born with a golden opportunity to be an alcoholic. My father has been in recovery since June 2003. His father drank at least as much as he did. My Dad's Dad cut way down on his drinking in his late forties/early fifties. (in the days before alcoholism became a disease and rehab was not yet a Hollywood status symbol) I don't think I ever saw him drunk. Maybe he hid it well. He died of cancer at 62. My mother's father was also a heavy drinker, possibly an alcoholic. He died of a heart attack at 59.

Do you think alcoholism might be in my genes? Maybe it just happened to show up in me as bipolar disorder. Maybe my father and grandfathers had some form of depression that they self-medicated with Iron City, Seagram's 7, and Canadian Club. A shot-and-a-beer has been known to calm the nerves and momentarily lift the spirits. Of course, that dependency thing and the fact that booze eventually depresses does hinder its effectiveness as an *anti*-depressant and mood stabilizer.

I started drinking near the end of my senior year of high school (late by alcoholic standards) and hit it hard throughout college. But my family history and my fanatic desire for physical fitness kept me wary. Somehow, by the grace of God, I kept from getting addicted. It could have easily happened and would have complicated the bipolar disorder I didn't realize I was already dealing with.

I would drink with friends, just looking to have a good time. And we did. But many of those times I was also unknowingly self-medicating. I was not diagnosed with depression until I was 26, but from the age of 18 I would drink two or three times a week in search of some relief from the agitation, frustration, moodiness, guilt, and obsessive thinking that I did not yet know to be bipolar disorder. I knew that something was not right. What a pain in the butt I must have been to the people around me. Why did they stick around? (If you have bipolar disorder that might be a good question to ask yourself. Those people sticking with you just might see something valuable that you are missing. Something good about you that makes them want to be with you.)

I was first prescribed medication for bipolar when I was 26, but I wanted to get off of it as soon as possible. That ended up being much sooner than my doctors thought wise. After sixteen months, I threw the meds away against their advice. For the next four years I used alcohol off and on, but never very much. I got back on medication for good in 1994.

There are many medications that are used to treat bipolar disorder. You can work with your doctor to find the one(s) that are best for you.

It took much trial and error, but my doctor and I finally found a combination that is unbelievably effective for me. I take Zoloft and Lamictal every day – and likely will for all of the rest of my days. They are not treatments for alcoholism, but the relief I get from them keeps me from feeling a need for alcohol. Also, from the day I started taking medications to treat bipolar disorder, I made – and have kept – a commitment not to mix meds with booze. (Thank God for making me a fitness fanatic. If I had not quit booze, then by the time my mind got relief from bipolar, I may well have already wrecked my body.)

I have not had a drink of alcohol in over 14 years and it is not difficult to stay away from it. In fact, I have absolutely zero need or desire for it. By the time I gave it up completely, it had actually lost any beneficial effect. Rather than lifting my spirits, one beer would make me feel sort of blue and drowsy. That wasn't what I wanted. And I never needed any chemical to make me depressed. My brain could handle that task *sua sponte* (that's legalese for 'on its own').

Regarding the question of self-medicating with booze versus taking the drugs that have been researched and demonstrated to help treat bipolar disorder, the answer is a no-brainer. Take the drugs. You and your doctor may not immediately find the medication(s) that is most effective for you, but the search will be worth it.

Bipolar is tough, but it does not wreck the body the way booze does. My grandfathers lived to 62 and 59. I intend to live just as long – as both put together! Take a look at Genesis 6:3. I'm claiming that.

"give thanks in all circumstances."
1Thessalonians 5:18 (New Living Translation)

CHAPTER 13

GUILT AND THE PRESENCE OF GOD

Even when I am overcome with legitimate guilt for my sin, I can boldly enter the Presence of my God and know His joy. This is, of course, not only true for a person who has bipolar disorder, but for all believers. The difference for me is that the guilt is extreme to the point of incapacitating. The heavier the burden that is lifted, the greater the experience of the love of God.

No, God does not love me any more in that moment than He loves any other sinner wildly seeking forgiveness. But I do believe that my experience of that love may be more profound because my experience of the guilt is so maddeningly extreme.

God does not want us to have to experience that extreme measure of guilt. It may even be a sin for me to persist in that guilt after confessing my sin. It is a denial of God's forgiveness which He desires for us to embrace immediately. But even though my stubborn, sinful guilt is not what He desires, He turns it into a blessing (Blessed with Bipolar) of a greater awareness of the magnitude of His love.

Don't be so stubborn as I have been. Don't push to know the extremes of guilt in the hope of getting the blessing. Bask daily in His presence and you'll know the love without so much of the senseless pain.

It is foolish to think that because we have sinned we are cut off from entering the loving presence of God. That is not the way He works.

The thief on the cross next to Jesus deserved to be there and he knew it. He had no time left to change his ways and live a life worthy of heaven. He was minutes from completing his life's journey to hell when he said to the other thief, " 'Don't you fear God even when you have been sentenced to die? We deserve to die for our crimes, but this man hasn't done anything wrong.' Then he said, 'Jesus, remember me when you come into your kingdom.' " (Luke 23:40b, 41-42) How did Jesus respond? "What, now, at the last minute you ask? Maybe if you had some time to prove yourself?" No. Jesus said without hesitation, "Today you will be with me in paradise." (Luke 23:43)

The thief, after a full life of sin and ignoring God, was embraced into God's Presence after breathing <u>one</u> genuine breath of true repentance.

We don't have to punish ourselves before we can be permitted back into God's presence. Christ took the punishment we deserve and He wants us back in His presence immediately – long before we feel like we deserve his loving-kindness, mercy, and forgiveness. In truth, we don't deserve it. Never can deserve it. And, praise God, He doesn't expect us ever to earn it. That's grace. That's love. That's God. Now, just accept it . . . It'd be a sin not to.

God's eagerness to forgive, however, does not mean that there is no consequence for my sin. When I am in the midst of (for example) lusting over a woman (or a mere image of a woman), I am choosing to build a wall between God and me. God does not withdraw His love. I turn away from it. I know I am sinning as I stare at that image and burn with lust and fantasy. And I keep on knowingly burning, lusting, and sinning. Feeling the guilt even in the moment that I lust, knowing that I will not long from now confess, and cry out for God's forgiveness. And, still, I persist, knowing that I am hurting the God who loves me more than I can imagine. The God who loves me even as I sin. (Would you believe that there are times when the Holy Spirit who dwells inside of me will play a worship song in my head as I lust? He is that jealous with love for me – and you.)

It makes no sense to believe that when I repent after a deliberate and knowing choice to disregard my God so persistently – and for no short time – that He instantly tears down the wall that I have built between Him and me. Instantly. That kind of love is foolish from the human perspective. But even the foolishness of God is greater than the wisdom of man (1 Corinthians 1:25)

What is more foolish is my insisting on beating myself over the head after God has run to me like the prodigal's father, torn down the wall, and is standing right in front of me – arms wide open – yearning for me to embrace Him.

Will I lust again after knowing the unmerited, undeserved love of God so profoundly? Am I a man?

Will God love me still? Is He God?

"There is nothing in all creation that can separate us from the love of God." (Romans 8). When I read this passage I believe it tells us that in the midst of our sin – before we repent – God still loves us as much as ever. At those moments we are not separated from His love. We are refusing it.

Repentance and God's forgiveness does not always result in me feeling His presence. That does not mean that I am not forgiven or that He is not with me. God's reality is not dependent upon my feelings. And the solution is not to keep beating myself up over a sin from which I have already repented. So, how can I be assured that God is with me if I don't feel Him here, if I don't sense His love?

Praise!

I have heard it preached that "the Lord inhabits the praises of His people." My immediate interpretation of that teaching was, "When we praise Him, God shows up."

Wrong.

God is omnipresent. He is with us all of the time. Our praise does not bring God into our presence or take us into His. He is always already here with us, and we, as Paul says (Ephesians 2:6), are already seated with Christ in the heavenly realms.

Our praise does not change God. He is the same yesterday, today, and tomorrow. (Hebrews 13:8) Our praise changes us. Praise makes us present to the fact of God's constant Presence. Our praise focuses us on the fact that He is always present and dwelling within us in the Holy Spirit.

When we praise God we come alive in, and to, the Presence of God inhabiting our praises. And we are changed.

What does all of this mean for the person who has bipolar disorder? There is an immediate, simple, though not easy, way out of the depression, irritation, agitation and guilt. If we can find the soundness of mind and spirit to praise God in the midst of our agonized emotions, we must and will be comforted and strengthened. I know from experience that it is nearly impossible to praise God in the throes of bipolar pain. I also know from experience that it is impossible to stay in that level of pain when I somehow _do_ find the courage to praise God.

There seems, in those moments of futility and mental torture, to be nothing to praise. Nothing worthy. The most natural response for the believer in that sort of pain is to say, "God, you had the power to stop this. You, all-powerful God, let this happen!" And there is real, and even understandable, temptation to curse God.

But He is still God. Still, the omnipotent Creator-King of the universe. My Creator. He is still pure Wisdom and pure Love. And, in His Wisdom which is beyond my understanding, He is always lovingly at work for my best. Even in the pain and suffering. He is worthy. Always.

I want to reach the point where bipolar pain immediately triggers me to praise God. I am not there yet. It is not a natural response. But I know that praising God is an all-out, warring attack on my despair, agitation, and guilt.

I am not saying that a simple "Hallelujah" brings me instant joy out of agony. It might. But it is more likely that I will have to get wild with prolonged worship even though it is the last thing in this world I feel like doing. But that may well be the key. In those moments, I desperately need to get out of this world – and into the very heaven-presence of God. And the only way I know to do that is to deliberately force myself into prolonged, wild, loud, fists-in-the-air worship. No damned demon of bipolar disorder can withstand a mad, Godly-warrior attack like that. He must flee in the Name of Jesus like a barking dog with no bite.

And if you do have bipolar disorder, then you are crazy enough to praise God with all your might, dancing undignified as King David in full sight of anyone who may care to risk a shot at wonder. You have probably gotten just as wild with far less reason in a filthy beer-soaked barroom. Do it for God, as goofy and long as necessary, and the depression will dwindle. The soul-wrenching anger will cease. And the guilt of false-condemnation will have to go.

We _always_ have instant access to the presence of God – no matter our sin. Repent. Release the stubborn guilt that Christ forgave on the Cross. Praise.

And know the all-loving joy of God. If the joy of the Lord is our strength (Nehemiah 10:8) and our praise brings Him joy, then we know that when we praise Him, He strengthens us. Do it and be set free!

Praise God and you will know His presence. Know His presence and you will be capable of nothing other than praise. Maybe even flopping-onto-your-knees, crying-out-loud praise.

*"I don't care about poison.
I don't care about fiery darts.
I don't care how rough the road is.
Show me where it starts."*
           - Bob Dylan (1980)

CHAPTER 14

"DEALING WITH" AUTHORITY

Getting screwed over presents a special challenge to a Christian who has bipolar disorder. A challenge that I have failed as often as not. Maybe more.

As John Cougar Mellencamp sang (1983), "I fight authority. Authority always wins/ I been doin' it since I was a young kid/ I've come out grinnin'. "

Except there came some times when it was not so funny. I lost jobs. I got hurled out of law school. I was over forty years old. And scripture commands (not *suggests*) that I work at dealing with the screw-over more effectively. In fact, scripture commands that I not just work at it, but that I get it done.

On a Saturday night in February 2008, Jeff Leake, senior pastor at Allison Park (Pennsylvania) Church of the Assemblies of God, started in with one of those sermons that has me leaning forward with my chin in my hands, staring at the floor, and thinking, "Okay, now, how much of this can I live with and how much of this just ain't for me?" I still have those moments. I examine almost everything before taking it hook, line, and sinker.

So, right there from the Saturday evening altar, Pastor Jeff hit me with this:

> "Everyone must submit himself to the governing authorities, for there is no authority except that which God has established. The authorities that exist have been established by God. Consequently, he who rebels against the authority is rebelling against what God has instituted, and those who do so will bring judgment on themselves." (Romans 13:1-2)

> "Therefore, it is necessary to submit to the authorities, not only because of possible punishment but also because of conscience." (Romans 13:5)

> "Submit yourselves for the Lord's sake to every authority instituted among men." (1Peter 2:13a)

> "Slaves, submit yourselves to your masters with all respect, not only to those who are good and considerate, but also to those who are harsh." (1Peter 2:18)

And my brain cracked back, "Yeah, that's a good guideline, but there are some times when you have to stand up and fight. If they're wrong, somebody's gotta tell'em or things will never change." And I felt obligated to be the one doing the telling. But those verses from Paul and Peter bugged me. Pastor Jeff was talking to me and I needed to listen.

Bipolar has something to do with the fact that I have struggled with authority – but not everything. There are some authorities who do not exactly dispose one toward submission. I ran brute-force into one of them in the form of my first semester torts professor (hereinafter referred to as "The Tort") in law school.

I did not expect law school to be easy and I did not expect law school professors to be sweetie-pie-honey-bunches. I expected that I would be required to be extremely well-prepared for every class (better prepared than in my graduate psychology program) and that none of my responses to interrogation would go unchallenged by the aforesaid Sweetie-Pies. And The Tort did not disappoint me.

It was my section's very first law school class session and The Tort let us know in no uncertain terms that his would be a no-nonsense training camp. In fact, he did so almost without any terms.

I arrived for the 9:00am class at 8:50. I'm not always on time, let alone ten minutes early, but I was not going to be late for my first class, especially given the rumor mill grindings regarding The Tort.

When I arrived The Tort was already pacing, almost prowling as if to pounce, around the room. He did not look like he had ever played the game, but he reminded me of a football coach all jacked-up just before kickoff, cracking with snarl and spit. That put him and me already off to a bad start without either of us having uttered a sound. (I firmly believe – from hot experience and cold-critical observation – that all football coaches at every level are a bit insane, a little too self-important, and not to be entirely trusted, Tony Dungy excluded. Considering those traits, I might have made a good one.)

As The Tort twitched, tapped, and eagerly bounded around the room, he kept quickly snatching glances at the clock on the classroom wall.

The Tort was up to something.

Students rushed in seconds before 9:00 and the suddenly grinning Tort fiendishly shut the door. Immediately, before The Tort could turn, the door shot open with a breathlessly hurried student. She did not get far. "I'll see ya Wednesday!" the Tort smartly snapped. His whole being was written with glee. Zip. The door opened again. "I'll se ya Wednesday!" And a cringing, sighing young lady disappeared behind the door now closed in her face. Glee. Pure glee for The Tort. He had been living for this since the previous year's first day of class.

The Tort was halfway to the podium when the door opened again. "Wednesday. 9 o'clock. Don't be late." He could not contain himself. The door opened and closed a couple more times before all the students on the wrong side got the message.

The Tort finally reached the podium and needlessly proclaimed, "If you want to attend class, get here on time. Class starts at 9. After that, nobody gets in and nobody gets out until we're done. In six years of teaching nobody has ever entered my class late and nobody has ever left early. If I've got to be here for fifty minutes, so do you!"

Believe it or not, I had no problem with that. It was law school. If we ever became lawyers and had to appear in court, the judge would demand that we be on time – even if he wasn't. Once we knew the rules and the consequences it was odd how easy it became to get to class on time. I even came to appreciate The Tort's "closed door" terrorism when students started to make a habit of walking five minutes late into the lectures of the less jihadi Sweetie-Pies.

The Torts hard-nosed tactics did not end with closing the door in the faces of latecomers. And, believe it or not again, I came to appreciate a fair portion of that. The Tort was demanding, but, again, it was law school. It needed to be demanding.

The Tort forced us to be prepared by putting people on the spot with rigorous, rapid-fire questioning about the cases we should have read, studied, analyzed, and re-read with the help of any study guide the school had subtly declared out-of-bounds. (If they did not want us to use them, they should not have let them be sold in the campus bookstore. But a buck is a buck. And, as we all know, tuition hardly covers the cost of lighting our institutions of higher legal learning, let alone paying the Sweetie-Pies.)

The Tort called on students hoping to find somebody who didn't have a clue. Most times, it was none too difficult. And nobody got off with answering just one question. Whether you answered correctly, incorrectly, or incoherently, there was sure to follow an abrupt "Why?," "What if?," or "So what?" And then a hypothetical shift in the facts of the case to force you to apply the law rather than simply memorize a stock answer to a predictable question. And responding to The Tort with a sad-eyed and pathetic, "I don't know," simply let The Tort know that it was time to swoop in on the road-kill. When anyone pleaded one of those pitiable "I don't knows," The Tort chomped, "Yes, but if you did know, what would you say?"

I have to admit – that's pretty good. We were law students. Why should he let us off the hook? What good would it do us if The Tort let us get away with an "I don't know?" He forced us to prepare and once we got to class – no matter how prepared we were – he forced us to think. It was fifty minutes in the cross-fire of rapid, vigorous, non-stop question and answer on matters that we scarcely could read, let alone understand. And you never knew when your turn alone on the battle front might come up and your dearest classmates would be relieved to see you taking the beating they had coming.

I appreciated it. I hated it. I was exhilarated and cranked-up by it. And I couldn't wait for it to be over. But it served me well and I had no problem with The Tort forcing us to work hard.

My problem was with The Tort's daily practice of humiliating people. He laughed at people's accents, ridiculed their former professions, insulted their previous education, and demeaned everything from their names to their haircuts, their clothes, their politics, and any other degradable attribute that popped into The Tort's mind.

It took no special talent for a law professor to be able to belittle a class of first semester students (1L's). There was no reason to suspect that any of us had any idea of what we were doing. 1L's don't know the law. In fact, when it comes to law, they don't even know how to read. And we were trying to decipher the ancient secret code of laws, facts, issues, reasoning, and decisions as they had been written by appellate judges. The Tort's success at humiliating us was about as grand an accomplishment as it would have been for a life-long Iranian to prove that we shamefully did not know Farsi.

It was law school. I expected to have to work hard. But it was not the marines. I quietly put up with The Tort's 'shame and destroy' style of teaching through August, September, and October. But as the Miami heat subsided, bipolar began to simmer.

When I was 16 I tolerated my football coaches and their ranting insults about a game that has no real consequences. I said nothing when a coach grabbed my facemask, shook my head, and screamed curses into my face from three inches away – all for the crime against humanity of blocking the wrong body across the line from me. I was a kid and he was my coach. At 16, that put him once step below god in my eyes. I kept my mouth shut and my fists on my hips. (At 26, I would have driven that coach into the dirt. Today, at 46, this Christian man would turn the other cheek – once.)

But I was not 16 in law school. I was 38, just like The Tort – and he was starting to look more and more like a soft-around-the-gut football coach who maybe talked a tougher game than he had ever played.

On a Friday in early November 2000, The Tort got a little surprise. He and one of my fellow students, Mr. Finnegan, went a few rounds over the facts, issues, and rulings of a case that we were studying. Finnegan stuck to his guns. I don't remember whether Finnegan was right and it doesn't matter. He believed that he was right and The Tort could not convince him otherwise. Finnegan was wise to stand his ground. It would not have been beyond The Tort to knowingly and adamantly take up the wrong position just to get Finnegan to cave and then laugh in his face.

I had seen it before. It didn't bother me much. The Tort was forcing Finnegan to defend his position. Nothing that Finnegan would not have to do daily if he ever became a lawyer.

The Tort moved on. There were other pigeons to b.b. gun off of the church roof. But as The Tort took shots at another student, he suddenly roared, "Mr. Finnegan, what do you think you're doing?!"

My head popped up out of its case-law cramming trance and I heard Finnegan moan, "I gotta yak." I looked to my left and saw him staggering down the ramp, looking like a gut-rotting ghost.

The Tort roared on. "Mr. Finnegan you are not going to leave this room!"

Finnegan kept walking.

"Nobody leaves my class. Mr. Finnegan, go back to your seat."

Sell your books at World of Books!

Go to sell.worldofbooks.com and get an instant price quote. We even pay the shipping - see what your old books are worth today!

Inspected By:Maria_Osornio

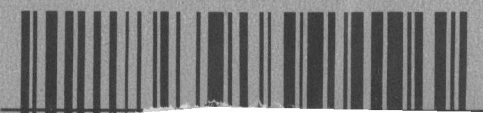

Finnegan said nothing and, just like any man who had to puke, he completely ignored The Tort.

I smirked in The Tort's direction, laughing my butt off on the inside. His ridiculous bluff had been called and his pride exposed as insecurity. For a split-second, he stood there naked with the whole class staring in wonder at what he might do next.

The Tort forced an anxious smile that said, "Man, I can't let them think that I've lost command." It didn't work. I wondered how well The Tort could take a punch. "Mr. Finnegan is going to regret this," he protested, "He should not have left this class. I expect all of you to stay here until I say that class is over. If you're sick, don't come. Use one of your absences. Don't come in here if you're sick," he said, the anger mounting. "Stay home. I don't want you coming in here and having to interrupt class because you're not smart enough to stay home when you're sick." The Tort was now ranting. And I was getting a little revved up myself.

"Mr. Rivas," The Tort demanded, "Take Mr. Finnegan's books and put them outside the door. I'm not letting him back in here. You leave, you don't get back in."

Rivas grinned and timidly carried Mr. Finnegan's books to the door. He did not look good.

The Tort had now lost control and I wasn't real happy with being yelled at like a child by a man my own age.

"If you have to vomit," The Tort raved, "Do it in your hands."

Suddenly, my face mask was being shaken and there was a lunatic football coach screaming curses three inches from my nose. But I wasn't 16 anymore.

I pushed my chair back hard and stood up in the middle of my row, halfway back in the room, smack in front of The Tort. I glared at him for an instant, turned, and took a step to my left. "Mr. Ya'Zhynka," The Tort roared, "What are you doing!?"

"I'm taking one of my absences," I growled and headed for the door...

The Tort screamed as I reached the end of the row, "Don't do this!"

I kept moving and started down the ramp.

"Mr. Ya'Zhynka, stop! This isn't going to be good for you."

I hit the bottom of the ramp, turned to leave, and heard The Tort say, "You don't want to go out that door." It was half demand and half plea. I paused, turned around, and started walking across the front of the room without saying a word. I looked The Tort in the eye, sneered and nodded as I passed him, and kept walking toward the door on the other side of the room as if to say, "You don't want me to go out _that_ door... I'll go out _this_ one."

The Tort warned, his tone moderating, "This isn't going to do you any good." I kept striding angrily for the door.

"Why are you doing this?" The Tort pleaded.

I stopped, incredulous at the possibility that anybody would not understand why I was refusing to put up with this garbage. I turned around and jabbed my fist toward Mr. Finnegan's seat. "Because that man was **sick** and you tried to humiliate him!" I barked.

"So, why do you have to leave the class?"

"There was no need for you to treat him like that and I'm not going to put up with it. Who do you think you are?"

"He shouldn't have come . . . if he was going to have to leave," The Tort contended weakly.

"Yeah, but he did and then he got sick. So what?"

"Do you want to go back and get your books," The Tort offered, trying to keep me in the room.

"I'll get 'em after class," I said with disgust.

"You're going to have to see me in my office right after class," The Tort directed.

"And if I don't—?" I smarted off.

The Tort's tone suddenly went soft. "Just make sure you come," he said. And I turned and went out the door.

Instead of going back to my room in the campus motel, I decided to sit in the breezeway between the law school and the law library and wait there until the end of The Tort's class to go back and get my books. My sitting and waiting, however, was interrupted by a lithium side effect – frequent urination. I went to the men's room and as I finished obliging the demands of my medication, I turned away from the urinal and was stunned. The Tort was leaning against the sink, arms folded across his chest, and staring at me. "You can't challenge me in my class," he scolded.

I could not believe what I was seeing and hearing, but I didn't stay stunned long. As I zipped up, I stared back and smirked, "So, you come in here and confront a man when he's got his (penis) in his hands."

The Tort and I barked backed and forth. The words were similar to what was said in class, but I was angrier and louder. Being challenged and scolded while urinating seems to do that to me.

A second year law student, who had the misfortune of needing to urinate shortly after I did, tried to rescue me. "C'mon, man," he urged, "you don't need this."

The Tort cracked, "No, no, leave him alone. Let him hit me."

I cocked my head at an angle, raised my eyebrows, and twanged-and-sang sarcastically, "I-I-I'm not going to hit you . . . professor . . . That would be insane."

And as we barked at each other, The Tort and I heard the unmistakable growling moans of Mr. Feingold puking into a men's room commode.

"Listen to that!" I yelled at The Tort as we stared each other down at close range, "Did you want him to do that in class?!"

That put an end to the "debate" and I headed for the door.

And The Tort said, *almost* apologetically, "Do you want to go back to class?"

That surprised me. "You'll let me go back to class?" I asked quietly.

The Tort nodded and I returned to class without further incident. I did meet with him in his office and we were both much more subdued. I agreed to take any possible future complaints to him privately, outside of class. My point had been made and The Tort knew that there was only so much that I would stand for. I believed there would be no further need to challenge him in class, so, I agreed to deal with any concerns privately. And The Tort never filed any complaint against me with the Law School. (I was expelled over four months later on the day the Law School Dean learned that I have bipolar disorder and received false allegations about me. That's a long, long story that ended in front of The Federal Circuit Court of Appeals in Miami, Florida)

I never had to confront The Tort again. He moderated his tone and I earned an "A." He eventually told an investigator from the United States Department of Education that I was a model student. And I told my friends that after our confrontation I had nothing but respect for him. (That sometimes happens after two men finally fight it out with each other.)

The Tort and I ended on good terms, but I know that if I had not walked out of his classroom on that early November morning, nothing would have changed. I no doubt could have handled the crisis better, but walking out was imperative.

Fast forward seven years to Allison Park Church and the preaching of Senior Pastor Jeff Leake. He starts in with the scriptural command to submit to authority and instantly The Tort, a few football coaches, and several former bosses are doing a return engagement in my brain – the bipolar one.

"Okay, Lord, you want me to submit to guys like this?! C'mon, now, Man. These were raging tyrants and incompetents. I gotta put up with _that_?! . . . Nah, I know you want me to stand up to that – for the good of everybody else, right?"

I tried to tell myself that I did not have to take those verses literally all the time. There had to be exceptions. But those verses from Peter and Paul had me bugged. When God gives a command, He means it and He expects it to be carried out. There is no question about the need to _literally_ submit to Him _all the time_. And I knew that, yes, God had, indeed, included raging tyrants and incompetents in that command when He said, "Slaves, submit yourselves to your masters, not only to those who are considerate, **but also to those who are harsh.**" (1 Peter 2:18, emphasis added)

Pastor Jeff had me annoyed. But I respect him as a spiritual leader. In fact, I once told him that I thank God that He has given me a spiritual leader to whom I can feel comfortable submitting. But I was bugged, nonetheless, and I knew that I had to deal with the command to submit in a way that would please God.

I was not too high on the idea. The Tort was "cuttin' a rug" in my brain and a snaggle-smooth boss was sneering live ammo. I was twitching inside and shifting in the pew. "All right, all right! I can feel it God. You don't have to shout. I'm convinced. I'll listen. I don't have to like it, but I will listen. But if you're gonna expect me to submit to tyrants, then you're gonna have to show me how to do it."

As Pastor Jeff spoke and I listened, ideas started to come to me about the meaning of submission and how to do it. At first, I did a little Bill-Clinton-type parsing of words to try to find a loophole or a legalistic way of technically obeying the command without really having to submit. It went something like this, "Hmmm, can I submit to authority? Well, God, that depends on what the meaning of the word 'to' is." As much as I admire the impeached former President, that was not going to get it done.

So, between what Pastor Jeff Leake preached and what was going on in my head while he preached, God gave me the following plan which has made me more "comfortable" with submitting. It may never be easy. It goes hard and fast against my stubborn rebel grain, but I can do this plan and be at peace with it.

These are the notes I took during the Saturday night service at Allison Park Church on February 17, 2008:

"DEALING WITH A CHALLENGING AUTHORITY FIGURE"

- It's God's will for me to submit to authority.
- Whatever authority there is in my life, God has put there.
- It pleases God for me to submit.
- The joy of the Lord is my strength – when I please Him, He strengthens me.
- I am not required to agree with authority.
- I can respectfully tell authority that I disagree.

- If I comply and the authority's plan fails, the failure is not my responsibility.

As important as it has always been to me to stand up to authorities when I believe they are wrong or, worse, mistreating people, it is far more important for me to please God. The realization that it pleases God for me to submit to authority made me see the value in it. If it is what God wants me to do, then it is a good thing - and good for me. It may not feel good, but I trust that God is using it for my good and strengthening me as I obey Him.

Submitting does not mean agreeing?! Hallelujah! If God does not expect me to _agree_ with a bad leadership command, then it becomes at least a little easier for me to follow it.

There is nothing in God's command to submit that says that I am not permitted to let the authority figure know that I disagree with him, but if I cannot find a way to do it _respectfully_, then it is best for me to keep my mouth shut and just follow his direction. If I do diligently and well what I am told to do, then the possible failure of the authority's plan is not my responsibility. I can live with that, knowing that I have done my duty. I have obeyed God's command to submit to authority.

It is NEVER going to be easy for me to submit to a boss, professor, or pastor when I think he is out of line (Submitting to a police officer is no problem for me. One night in jail was enough for a lifetime). But this plan makes it more palatable. It is possible because I know that it pleases God. And if He commands it, then He will equip me to do it. That sounds good, but I know myself well. God is going to have to take over and do it in me. (Now, that last sentence just caught me by surprise. Have I not yet fully submitted to the Boss of bosses?)

So, with this new understanding of submission, how would I now handle The Tort's rant of, "You don't leave my class. If you have to vomit, do it in your hands." I'd sit there and take it. And then I would sue him for false imprisonment – just like he taught me to do. For the Courts of the United States are also a governing authority – to which even The Tort must submit.

"Nebuchadnezzar said to them, 'Is it true Shadrach, Meshach, and Abednego, that you refuse to serve my gods or to worship the gold statue I have set up? I will give you one more chance. If you bow down and worship the statue I have made when you hear the sound of the musical instruments, all will be well. But if you refuse, you will be thrown immediately into the blazing furnace. What god will be able to rescue you from my power then?'

"Shadrach, Meshach, and Abednego replied, 'O, Nebuchadnezzar, we do not need to defend ourselves before you. If we are thrown into the blazing furnace, the God whom we serve is able to save us. He will rescue us from your power, Your Majesty. But even if He doesn't, Your Majesty can be sure that we will never serve your gods or worship the gold statue you have set up.'"

Daniel 3:14-18 (NLT)

CHAPTER 15

FORGIVENESS

"For a Christian, the only appropriate response to the words, "I'm sorry," is the words, "I forgive you." I had no argument against that biblical logic when it was expounded by an old girlfriend of mine. And it messed me up.

I have bipolar disorder, remember? That means I sometimes blow my stack. And when I blow my stack, there are always "I'm sorry's" and "I forgive you's" that must be said. And many of those times the last thing I want to do is apologize and/or forgive.

Saying, "I'm sorry," has come more naturally to my bipolar disposition than has saying, "I forgive you." In the past I was bombarded with an unrealistic measure of bipolar guilt over slight, and even imagined, offenses. I would get so depressed in that guilt that there would be no getting free without an apology to man and God. So I did it because I could not stand the guilt. However, there were often many apologies for the same offense because I could not accept forgiveness or forgive myself. It was, indeed, bipolar.

Now, after many teachings on God's perfect and immediate forgiveness, I am able to let go of the guilt the moment that I am convicted of my sin and repent.

The impact of being able to receive forgiveness has been life-changing. I no longer waste hours and days, bathing in my self-absorbed guilt. There was something prideful about it, as if I believed that I were actually above committing the rotten behavior that had so pounded my conscience. The guilt was like telling myself that I really ought to be good enough to earn my own salvation. There was something self-serving and self-satisfying in lashing that whip to my own flesh. Guilt may, in fact, have been my way of trying to earn my salvation. It never worked. Never could. It just led to more sin. And I wasted so much time feeling guilty long after God had forgiven me.

It took many years – long after my salvation – to accept the hard fact that I am a sinner through and through and that Christ took the penalty for _all_ of my sin – past, present, and future. And that I _needed_ Him to do it because I am completely incapable of doing it myself. How can I earn my way to heaven if the penalty for my sins is an eternity in hell? Finally, I stopped trying to do the impossible.

Humbling myself to the point of saying, "I'm sorry," was much easier than humbling myself to the point of saying, "Christ paid it all and God has forgiven my sins completely." Even my pride. When

Jesus went to that Cross, He left no more penalty for me to pay, regardless of my errant and pride-filled desire to suffer for my own sins.

Therefore, I now repent and declare, "In Jesus' Name, according to the Word of God, 'There is no condemnation for those who are in Christ Jesus.' " And I immediately accept His forgiveness and move on.

Forgiving others has not come as naturally to my bipolar personality as did apologizing. When I pop my manic lid with anger, I feel one-hundred percent righteously indignant. "They were wrong and I'm gonna tell'em straight in the face," I rage wild-eyed, loud, and veins-bulging with all six foot four inches and 215 pounds of my mood-swung self. (Of course, that lands me not only having to forgive, but also apologize.)

I had to learn forgiveness because God commands it and because anger was eating away at my soul. It is only by the grace of God that such intense and persistent anger did not damage my body. A stroke or heart attack could well have hit by now. Instead, my blood pressure is 120/80, my good cholesterol is off-the-charts high, my bad cholesterol is low, and my blood sugar is normal. All by the grace of the Great Physician.

The greatest challenge to my obedience to God's command to forgive came when I was immediately and unexpectedly expelled from law school without any opportunity to tell my side of the story. I was evicted from my room in the campus motel and forced to leave instantly under the threat of a police escort to Who-Knows-Where. And by 'instantly,' I mean, "right now!" - without so much as time to pack up my belongings. I was stunned and angry, but I did not explode as expected. In fact, the woman who courageously delivered the law school dean's letter of expulsion told police that I "responded calmly and left campus peacefully." That was not because I am such a mild-mannered, meek and lowly, little angel. I was too much in shock to respond at all.

My mind, body, and emotions shut down for several days. That was a good thing. I needed to focus on what I had to get done, not the least of which was making the twelve-hundred mile drive home from Miami to Pittsburgh with a kitten that I had never before put in a car. (She lay in her litter box and puked for the first two-hundred miles.) If the full emotional impact of the expulsion had hit me all at once and I did not go into shock, I probably would have spent some time in jail. I would have exploded – and the Metro-Dade police were right outside the door when the dean's letter was delivered.

I left campus, went to Delaney's bar in Hialeah, Florida, and danced like a madman. I suppose that a psychologist would call it denial. So what? It got me through the night without getting locked in a jail or psych ward.

I woke up the next morning in a room of the Holiday Inn at Pro Player Stadium, smack on the border of Dade and Broward counties halfway between Miami and Fort Lauderdale.

The expulsion letter had stated that the law school would pay for a night at the Holiday Inn and a flight "to your home in Philadelphia." (The helpfulness of that offer was limited by the fact that my home is in Pittsburgh) I have yet to understand the school's logic in expelling me for the unsubstantiated allegation of being an imminent threat to harm persons and property and, in the same instant, taking responsibility for putting me up in a hotel and placing me on-board a plane. If they believed that I was an imminent threat of physical harm, why would they knowingly and deliberately unleash me on a hotel full of unsuspecting vacationers and a plane full of innocent passengers? Something about that scenario just does not match up. Especially when you consider that nobody ever came forward to testify that they had heard me make threats or seen me commit any violence.[3] (The school's supposed 'star witness' actually ended up filing an affidavit stating that I had never made threats or harmed any persons or property.)

[You can, and will, draw your own conclusions about whether I should have been expelled, but you should know that the Dean of the Law School first learned that I have bipolar disorder no more than one day before he expelled me.[1]]

I woke-up half-sure that I was in the Holiday Inn. I was still in shock and wanted to stay there. My head was reeling from the largest dose of Zoloft I had taken in months and the bomb that had exploded in the middle of my life the night before.

"This really did happen," I thought, not trying to convince myself. I rolled over and pushed my face into a pillow. It wasn't going to go away, but I didn't have to deal with it – yet.

I had that damnable hangover feeling, though I _still_ had not had a drink in over six years. My head was filled with bruise-blue clouds like leftovers from a hurricane. I could still hear some thunder. I buried myself deeper in the quilts and went back to sleep.

If I were at home, I would have balled myself up in a 48 to 72 hour coma. Considering the other possibilities, it is not always a bad option, but on this day it was not one that I had. To my good fortune and chagrin, the Holiday Inn has a check-out time. I slogged heavy-headed into and out of the shower, dressed, and dragged myself sleep-walking to the front desk and out the door.

I was in no shape to drive from Miami to Pittsburgh and had nowhere else to go. I landed on the beach at Hollywood out of force of habit. I bumbled my way down the boardwalk in a trance that started to muster a little anger, when, bang! I got hammered over the head with a holy whisper, "You need to forgive those people."

"What?!" I flamed in my spirit. "Forgive them?! Do you know what they did to me? It hasn't even been a full day – and you want me to forgive them?!"

"You _need_ to forgive them," said the Holy Spirit.

"No," said I, "not now I don't."

I was walking more boldly now, my head still filled with the bruise-blue clouds – and a sudden flash of lightning. A little more anger starting to break the shock.

"You know that I expect you to forgive them," said the Holy Spirit. "Just like the Father forgives you."

"How can I forgive them?"

"Jesus died for your sins."

"Yes. Yes . . . he did. And I can never thank Him enough," I knew in my spirit.

"They are sinners," said the Holy Spirit.

I agreed.

"They need to be forgiven - and you . . . *need* to forgive them."

Somehow, by the grace of God, I was stopped dead in my tracks and the wind blew out of my chest. I threw back my head, raised my arms, and sighed, "Okay . . . but I don't *feel* like forgiving them. I don't *feel* forgiveness in my heart. And I'm not going to."

But I knew that I did have to forgive everyone who was involved in my expulsion – deans, professors, students, and all others of whom I was unaware. This would have been difficult had the blessing of bipolar disorder not previously led me through a number of "encounters" in which I had to forgive and be forgiven. But I still had more to learn about how to forgive when I did not feel the slightest forgiveness in my heart, mind, soul, or spirit.

"You don't need to feel it," said the Holy Spirit, "You need to *do* it."

I stood back and pondered that one for a second. "That sounds strange," I said, "And... maybe, like I can do it."

"Forgiveness is an act," the Holy Spirit instructed. "It's something you can _decide_ to do even if you don't feel it."

"Okay. I know I have to do this. I just didn't expect to have to do it so soon. It hasn't been twenty-four hours since they shoved me out without hearing even one word from me," I faintly protested. "They just threw me out. Immediately. Didn't care what I had to say. Didn't even ask."

"Yes. They were wrong," agreed the Holy Spirit. "That's why you have to forgive them."

"Now?"

"Look, I'm not gonna force you to do it. If you need to let it eat away at you a little longer, that's up to you."

I think I heard a smirk in there.

"I don't _feel_ any forgiveness," I gritted and frowned.

"You think I didn't know that before you ever thought about it?" the Holy Spirit grinned. "Do it – and sooner or later you'll start feeling it."

It was then that I remembered a teaching on forgiveness by Emmet Fox (1934, pp.175-176) that I had read seven or eight years earlier. It went something like this:

- Tell God that you forgive them.
- Release them from your anger.
- Pray for God to bless them.
- Keep it short. Dwelling on it too long will give the anger a chance to flare up

In that moment – right there on the beach – I said it in my spirit and may have even whispered it out loud like I was publicly talking to myself. "God, I forgive them. I forgive Dean (_____). I forgive Professor (_____). And I forgive (the students) who got me expelled. You want me to forgive them, Lord. I know. I forgive them, Lord, and I ask you to forgive me. Bless them, Lord. Bring them to know Christ as their Lord and Savior. I release them from my anger. Lord, take away my anger."

Emmet Fox also taught that if, after you forgive your debtor, the anger does flare up again, "bless the delinquent briefly and dismiss the thought." (1934, p.175). Do not forgive them again for the initial offense. That would be like saying that you had not forgiven them the first time. (1934, p.175)

I implemented the above procedure many times - and for a number of years – after I forgave St. Thomas University on the beach of Hollywood, Florida. Occasionally, several times a day. The anger flared often, but I ended up praying for my expellers nightly regardless of whether I was angry. It had something to do with that 'Love your enemies and pray for your persecutors' stuff. Even while I was suing them.

The lawsuit was not about revenge. I *did* forgive them on that beach at Hollywood the day after I got the boot. I did not sue to get back at them. I sued because I wanted to be fully compensated for what had been taken away from me. But, I must admit, I did enjoy the fact that I was making St. Thomas University School of Law spend some money defending themselves. On the other hand, they could have spared themselves that expense at any time by making a legitimate settlement offer. They chose, instead, to continue spending money on the lawsuit.

I did eventually start to *feel* forgiveness and God has taken away all of the anger.

I got expelled on the day the school learned that I have bipolar disorder. And the very next day, God used the resulting manic anger and depression to teach me a practical, real-life lesson about forgiveness. It is much easier now.

*"I know, O Lord, that your
 decisions are fair;
you disciplined me because I
 needed it."*
                    Psalm 119:75 (NLT)

CHAPTER 16

OPERATION SHUTDOWN

Several years ago, in the gasping-last-chance days of his major league baseball career, Pittsburgh Pirate outfielder Derek Bell coined the term "Operation Shutdown." He believed that he should be anointed in spring training as one of the team's everyday starting outfielders – regardless of his pre-season performance. When the question arose regarding whether Bell would, indeed, be a starter, he notoriously pronounced that if he had to actually *'win'* a starting job, he would go into "Operation Shutdown." By that he apparently meant that he would not give his best effort. Some later wondered how they would have noticed; after being handed the starting job, Bell promptly batted .173 with 5 homeruns and 13 RBI.

Operation Shutdown did not work out well for Derek Bell. His days in Major League Baseball ended abruptly thereafter. However, I have learned that there are times when shutting down the operation is the best thing I can do.

On August 6, 2008, forty-five pages worth of rough drafts of this document disappeared from my laptop computer. A heretofore unseen desktop appeared on my windows monitor. I thought nothing of it. There were still icons on the screen and I assumed that somehow the computer had merely changed the screen-saver.

I checked my email and a couple of other sites and decided to do something else (probably eat). But as I logged off I noticed that there did not seem to be the usual number of icons on the desktop. I was curious, but certainly not alarmed. I assumed that I could easily retrieve the old desktop and the full set of icons, folders, and documents would return. But . . . when I restarted the computer, the new and deficient desktop was still on the screen – a beautiful rural summer scene of God's green hills and crystal sky that made me wince.

I drew a deep breath, rubbed my hand across my cheek and lips, and – with calm now an effort – mumbled and grinned, "Okay, it's gotta be in there somewhere. It didn't just disappear."

I went into the control panel and clicked on "Recent Documents." "(Empty)." Uh-oh, not good. I clicked on "My Documents" and two folders appeared, "My Pictures" and "My Videos." Very bad. "My Documents" is where the forty-five pages of this rough manuscript had been stored in a folder titled "BBp." Yes, <u>Blessed with Bipolar</u>. I wasn't feeling it. The seeds of manic agitation had been sown.

"What in the (curse) is going on here?! I didn't do anything to make this (curse ing) thing disappear."

The situation cried out for Derek Bell. It was time for my own Operation Shutdown, but I just could not pull myself away.

I shut the computer off, waited a few seconds, and restarted it. Sometimes, I can trick it into giving me what I want. This wasn't one of those times. The screen lit up, the corporate jingle tune played... Same deficient desktop... with the rolling green screensaver that just happened to be named, "Blissful." "Yeah, ya (curse), I'll give ya a fistful of Blissful!"

Control Panel. Click. Recent Documents. "(Empty)." Click. My Documents. "Pictures." "Videos." No BBp. "(Curse! Curse! Son of a curse!)"

I told myself to stay calm. I tried to convince myself that the lost documents had to be in there somewhere. And, finally, I half-heartedly whispered, "God, put those documents back on this computer."

The bipolar would have exploded out of me right then and there, but, fortunately, I have near immediate access to some of the world's finest computer experts. Grandma Lucy (my mother) is an Assistant Administrator for the Pittsburgh Supercomputing Center at Carnegie Mellon University. Yes, at the age of 46, I called my mommy with a crisis. But my mommy ain't like every mommy. She earned her masters degree at retirement age and she assists computer geniuses - and my (curse) computer had just stolen 45 pages of semi-hard, half-decent work that I did not want to try to reproduce. So, I called my mommy.

I anxiously informed Grandma Lucy of my dilemma, my voice less than steady and making a large effort not to erupt. She said she would talk to the experts and call me back. I knew she would, so, I took another deep breath and tried to think of something other than the work that went into those 45 pages of second and third draft.

It was not easy. I could feel the bipolar man inside of me - whom no amount of lamictal and Zoloft can make completely go away - yearning to explode.

Grandma Lucy called within five minutes and gave me the instructions:

Go to Control Panel.
Click Display.
Click Desktop.
I sat down to the computer.
10 – 9 – 8 . . .
. . . and started clicking.
7 – 6 . . .
. . . Click. Final step.
5 – 4 . . .
. . . Click. Close Window. Close Control Panel . . . Same new (curse) deficient (curse) "Bliss" screen-saver.
3 . . .
"Okay, it didn't work. (curse). I'm gonna explode, " I growled. My fists balled up. My teeth clenched. I glared, glassy-eyed and seething, at the computer.

Deep breath. "Try it again," I slowly exhaled venom.

Control Panel. Display. Desktop. Click. Click. Click. "(<u>Curse</u> . . . <u>curse</u> . . . <u>mother curse</u>.)"

Screen–saver "Bliss." 3 -2 -1

POP! goes my steaming lid right into bipolar orbit with a blizzard of curses.

I pounded the kitchen table and growled forth a new language. "45 PAGES GONE! NOTHING GOES RIGHT!"

I caught myself, still ranting curses, and somehow chose not to jump up on my broken ankle against every natural manic instinct.

Unfortunately, my father was innocently standing in the line of fire and I yelled at him. I turned into an idiot, misdirecting my anger at the man who is the tangible love of God on earth to me. Just as my Dad was saying, "Rich, I didn't do anything –," I roared, "Yeah, what if I went out and dug up your (<u>curse</u>) lawn," equating his tireless, diligent work on the yard with my 45 lost pages.

I should have known better. I *do* know better. I should have gone into "Operation Shutdown" as soon as the computer went rogue and I felt bipolar-man rising up. I had felt the explosion building. I needed to get away from that computer, go outside, take a walk on my crutches, blast a Bob Dylan song and sing "Thunder On the Mountain" at the top of my lungs. Anything - pour a bucket of water over my head – anything to get my mind off of that computer and keep from exploding. And praise God through it all.

But Derek Bell was the farthest thing from my mind.

After yelling at my father, I hobbled and bounced and tripped up the steps, slammed my crutches on the floor, and went to bed at noon. Operation Shutdown – 10 minutes too late.

At times like this I need to realize that nothing is as important – in that moment – as avoiding an explosion and a downward spiral that could last five days. I need to take myself out of whatever it is that I am doing – no matter how important it may seem – and shut down my emotions before they rage. I need to take a deep breath and get away, take another deep breath, walk hard and fast, and pray until I think straight. It might take a long time. Calling my counselor quickly would be a good idea. I must stop the explosion.

My father took the laptop to Grandma Lucy at Carnegie Mellon University and the experts retrieved my documents. Somewhere, deep down I always knew that my 45 pages would be found, but somewhere else – not quite as deep down – I wanted to explode, and did.

I repented and spent the next 24 hours feeling guilty, childish, ungrateful, mean, and imbecilic. I needlessly whipped myself instead of receiving the forgiveness that I knew God had already granted. Pride said that I needed to take a beating first.

"God, I pray, show me when to shut it down. God, I surrender. Take control and shut me down so I do no harm."

*"The suffering you sent was good
  for me,
for it taught me to pay attention
  to your principles."*

Psalm 119:71 (NLT)

CHAPTER 17

BONE-BREAKING BLESSINGS

Two days ago I spent 45 minutes in quiet contemplation and brief intercession in the prayer chapel at Allison Park Church. I closed by praying in the Spirit (tongues) for a couple of minutes. The woman scheduled after me to continue the church's attempt at 24 hour / 7 day a week prayer in the chapel showed up seconds before I finished. I told her that she nearly caught me praying in tongues. If she had been a new believer, I would have looked like a raving madman who had little orientation to any kind of reality. And she would have cut out, thinking, "What in the name of nonsense have I gotten myself into now?" She understood and we had a good laugh. I asked God to anoint her prayer time and said good-bye.

I really should have left the building. But between the prayer chapel and my car was a makeshift gym that the church has thrown together for its teenagers and young people. That's where the trouble started.

For me, teen-age is a 26 year-old memory to which my bipolar brain sometimes says, "So what?" The heavy punching bag was verily crying out my name. "C'mon, Ya'Zhynka, I dare ya." I was not going to put up with that crap out of some lousy bag. So, I wound-up, leaped forward onto my left leg, and swung my right foot soccer-style and "take that!"smack into the mid-section of that yapping, arrogant, pansy bag.

Nineteen hours later I was looking at two cracks on an x-ray of my ankle. Football, street hockey, roller-blading, and a 26-mile marathon never caused me to break a bone. It took a nit-witted bipolar kick at a punching bag to get that done.

I am thrilled that I was only messing around when I kicked that bag. I would have felt like an idiot if I had broken my ankle in a fit of bipolar rage. It's much better to do it in a fit of bipolar goofball impulsivity.

My faith-informed experience of bipolar disorder, somehow, empowered me to understand this whole childlike scene in terms of blessing. Could it be that the Holy Spirit is using the writing of this book to train me to look for blessing in everything, not only bipolar disorder?

Things have changed. Two years ago my bipolar response to breaking my ankle would have been a cursing rampage. I would have been angry at myself, angry at the bag, angry at whoever put the bag there to tempt me in the first place, and, ultimately, angry at God (all anger is ultimately anger at God). But the

Holy Spirit used the loss of my lawsuit against St. Thomas University in December 2006 to change me. "Change" may actually be too mild a word. The Holy Spirit transformed me in the loss of that lawsuit.

During the lawsuit, I had imagined that the loss of it would be the loss of my last chance to have a life. I was suing because St. Thomas had expelled me from law school without a hearing and without any chance to be heard in my own defense. I owed $18,500 in school loans, had no job, and no chance to get accepted at another law school. As I think about it now, I realize that when I lost the lawsuit, I did lose my last chance to have the life I had hoped for. But I gained something so much greater – the lived understanding that I did not need to win the lawsuit and I did not need to have the life I had hoped for. In my loss, God proved that He really does, and always will, provide for all of my needs. And I realized that He always has. Always.

I lost the life I had hoped for, but I gained more of Christ. Didn't He say, "He who loses his life in this world shall find it?" Don't let that deal go down without you. You will never find one better. Having my emotions and outlook on life so magnificently transformed in the _loss_ of the lawsuit – something that I could not have previously imagined surviving – led to my discovering the many blessings of bipolar disorder.

So, yes, I do see breaking my ankle as a blessing. I do not doubt that you will think that I am making this up. That I am stretching this thing a bit too far. "Right, breaking your bones is a good thing. Everything's a blessing. Get off it, man." I can hear you.

Well, I admit it. I do now want to search for blessing in everything because I have seen God turn what seemed catastrophic into enlightenment, wonder, peace, and a changed man. I have seen God be at work for good in the greatly feared things in the life of one who loves Him, one who is called according to His purposes. I have seen God take what man intended for evil and turn it for good and the saving of lives. It has happened in me, in the loss of my lawsuit against the school that had hastily expelled me, and in bipolar disorder so extreme that it required seven emergency hospitalizations. So, yes, as odd as it may seem, I do now look for blessings in broken bones.

As soon as I wrote that last paragraph I got up from my table in the food court at Ross Park Mall to meet my father who had driven me there and was picking me up at 3:45. (sort of like the father of a teenager who had broken his ankle kicking a punching bag). Before I reached the door I saw a boy of 10 or 11 sitting beside two metal crutches with a sky blue cast on his leg. He looked up and we both smiled. Bipolar extrovert Ya'Zhynka was engaged. Richard the Introverted took a seat and waited to write about whatever was about to happen. (I've got the two of them a little more under my discipline now. But I do allow them some freedom.)

I asked the boy what had happened to his leg and he quickly responded, "I cut my Achilles tendon."

Whoa! I thought of athletes who had their professional careers ended by Achilles tendon injuries.

"How'd it happen?" I asked.

"I was riding my friend's electric scooter up a hill and it stopped. So, I put my foot down, ya know," He smiled, "like you would with a regular bike? But it had a kick-stand and it wasn't — It was down and it cut into my leg," He still smiled, all bright, blue-eyed like sunshine.

My eyes went wide as my jaw fell open, "Oh, man, that's bad. Was it severed, cut all the way through? (He knew what severed meant.)

"There was just a thread left." His eyes sparkled.

Every dream a 10 year-old boy has for his summer – swimming, baseball, bike-riding, a day or two at Kennywood Park riding the Thunderbolt, the Pittsburgh Plunge, and Raging Rapids – had been trashed in an instant. And his eyes still sparkled and his face still smiled through the whole conversation. The summer he dreamed about every winter afternoon while his teacher droned on about pronouns, participles, polar ice caps, and global warming had been blown away, but there was not one scintilla of a trace of bitterness or self-pity about him. I liked this kid.

"So, you had surgery?" (I was a little sensitive to that issue. My doctor had firmly warned me earlier that morning to keep the Darth Vader boot-cast on my broken ankle by saying, "You're going to live in that boot . . . If the bone doesn't move, you won't need surgery." I guess he assumed that if a 46 year-old man is screwy enough to kick an anchored heavy-bag, he might just be screwy enough to take off the boot-cast and run. I will behave . . . but my five-year-old nephew is coming to town from Nashville and with him arrives temptation to the screwy.)

The young boy gave the obvious answer to my needless question and added a stunner. He told me that he did have surgery and added, "They said if it had gone that much further (he held his index finger and thumb together), they would have had to amputate my foot."

My ankle didn't feel so broken anymore.

"You almost lost your foot?" I said in awe.

He nodded and grinned.

"How long will you have the cast on?"

"Six weeks."

I did not have the heart to say, "Just in time to go back to school," as if he had not considered that a thousand times.

I do not know what else is going on in that kid's life, but he is blessed with a beautiful outlook on life that some people go to their grave without attaining. Somehow, God is blessing him with that cut Achilles and if he puts it all in the hands of the Lord, God will turn this nearly tragic summer into a blessing for the rest of his life. He may even be inspired to author a piece of Christian non-fiction about it.

I asked the boy if I could pray for him and he shifted quizically at the out-of-place mid-mall request, then sat up straight, and grinned, "Sure." He might not have expected that I would break out in intercession right on the spot. "Jesus, heal this boy's Achilles tendon. Thank you for the healing you have already worked in him. And thank you that he didn't lose that foot."

The boy was a blessing to me. One I would have missed had it not been for the breaking of my ankle.

God also used the broken ankle to force me to take the rest I have needed - but would not have taken - from working-out. I have been pushing too far, too often. My body kept groaning, "I'm not 26." And I kept mindlessly pushing. I took a couple of days off, felt a little better, and went back to pushing and hurting several times. I was about to do it again when the ankle cracked. God's way of saying, "Your body needs a break, but you're not going to take it unless I break you." My shoulders, knees, and quadriceps feel better than they have in weeks. They thank my ankle.

Last week, prior to breaking my ankle, I said to my mother, "Y'know, I have had such great peace and joy for the past year-and-a-half . . . I'd like to get to the point where I know I would have that peace even if I had physical limitations that kept me from ever working-out again and I couldn't stay in shape. Could I still have this same peace?"

God has allowed me the chance to practice. I am on the 15 day disabled list and unsure of when I will be reinstated. So, God and I have a chance to prove our faithfulness to each other. Will I believe that He is working in and through this fractured ankle for my absolute best? Will I believe that in this He is providing everything I need? That He is all I need? That He is my peace and His joy is my strength – even if I cannot walk? Even if I – Oh no! – get fat?

So far, so good.

I will praise Him and He will come through and the whole experience will strengthen my faith for its next challenge. And I will have peace. And I will have joy. I trust the Lord to love me beyond anything I can imagine – even when He calls me into a time of suffering that He will use to win souls and give Him glory and bless me. When I am weak, then I am strong, for the Lord's strength is made perfect in my weakness.

Because I have recognized the blessings of bipolar disorder in and through its anguish, I can believe more fully that God will bless me richly in any adversity that I must face. And that is a blessing that I can transfer into every situation. A blessing that has transformed me and, I pray, will continue to be used by God to transform me until I truly take on the image of His Son.

How can I repay the Lord
  for all his goodness to me?
I will lift up the cup of salvation
  and call on the name of the
    Lord.
I will fulfill my vows to the Lord
  in the presence of all his people.

Precious in the sight of the Lord
  is the death of his saints.
O Lord, truly I am your servant;
  I am your servant, the son of
    your maidservant;
  you have freed me from my chains.

I will sacrifice a thank offering to
    you
  and call upon the name of the Lord.
I will fulfill my vows to the Lord
  in the presence of all his people,
in the courts of the house of the
    Lord —
  in your midst, O Jerusalem.

Praise the Lord.
                              - Psalm 116:12-19

CHAPTER 18

COMFORTING WITH THE COMFORT GIVEN

(2Corinthians 1:4)

—∭—

My neighbor is dying. He is 78. He has cancer of the pancreas. Three days ago his condition suddenly worsened drastically. He was taken by ambulance to the same hospital in which I was born.

As best I know, Joe, my neighbor, is unsaved. And he may not have much time left. Twenty years ago, when I was hospitalized in desperate condition, a man loved me enough to visit and witness. Now, it is my chance. And my responsibility.

I visited Joe today, believing that it would be the last time I would see him. When I learned of his deteriorating condition, I quickly went to the hospital. I wanted to delay, check the internet, maybe go to Ross Park Mall, and get to the hospital in the mid-afternoon. That seemed unwise. I decided to jump in the shower, change clothes and go. Then the thought hit me, "What difference will it make to get to the hospital all cleaned and pressed to find out that, while I was in the shower, Joe died." I left in yesterday's clothes, grime, and grease.

I was not surprised to find Joe frail and much weaker than the last time I had seen him – about three weeks ago. His wife had told me that he was dying so I was prepared to see him physically corrupted. I imagined him swollen with fluid and strangely discolored. When I entered his room I had a picture of death in my mind.

Joe looked better than the picture and, for a moment, I was pleased. I was stunned, however, by what dying is doing to his mind. He recognized his wife and me, but only briefly. At times, he seemed to be hallucinating. He had trouble speaking, not, it seemed, because of any physical disability, but because his brain wasn't getting the thoughts to his mouth. Out of nowhere, he rapidly mumbled to his doctor, "I walked a half-a-mile in the snow. I was determined . . . I'm incapacitated."

We get some snow in Pittsburgh, less than Buffalo, but never on June 24.

I didn't know whether Joe was joking about his physical deterioration, dreaming of some past adventure, or having a delusion. I told him again who I was and he said, "Oh. I called you Paul." Maybe he was thinking of my brother whose name is Peter.

Joe was lying there right in front of me, probably no more than a week from death, and I was cracking-ready to give bold witness. And I had no idea whether he was at all connected to reality.

Why had I not gone across the street a week earlier? Why had I not passionately said the things I was about to say back when I knew his mind was working? I had told myself that there would be another chance. That I would see him on his death bed and he would be desperate for Christ. I had not considered that Joe would not be lucid.

I held his left hand and said, "Joe, I'm going to pray with you." His eyes flashed for a second in a way that I hoped meant urgency. "Okay. Thank you." I leaned forward and put my head down close to the bed. "Joe, I want you to be with Jesus . . . because . . . I know you're struggling."

I paused. I was nervous. I searched for just the right words. Can you imagine?! The man was on his death and I was worried about looking like a crazed idiot. I quickly upbraided myself, "Just open your d_ _ _ mouth and speak."

"Joe, Jesus wants you to be with Him, but you have to ask Him into your life. Do you want to be with Him?" Joe was still.

"Jesus is the Son of God. He died on the Cross for our sins. Jesus loves you, Joe, and he wants you to be with Him." I paused. "Joe, do you want to give your life to Jesus? Do you give your life to Jesus?" He nodded so slightly and grunted what I desperately hope he meant, "Uh-huh, yes!"

I witnessed hard six inches from his ear – like I could have done a week earlier when I knew his mind was sound. I pray he had one last lucid moment.

Note:

Four days after I wrote the above-section I went to Allison Park Church for the end of the 9:00 Sunday service. (I like to worship at the end of the 9:00 service and then stay for the 11:00 service.) As the service ended, Jeff Leake, the Senior Pastor, called forward some leaders to pray individually with whomever so desired. I was not interested. No specific prayer need came to my mind. I wanted to sing along with the worship team, praise God, and simply dwell in His presence. That was not God's plan. There are times for dwelling and times to take charge.

I was not quite sure, but it felt like the Holy Spirit in me began to stir. One of the prayer leaders was standing alone and that voice in my spirit said, "Don't pass up an opportunity to have somebody pray for you." And I replied to that voice in my spirit, "Man, I don't have anything that I need prayer for right now. I just want to worship. Let me hang out with God."

And the Holy Spirit said in my spirit," Hey, dummy, don't pass up an opportunity to have somebody pray for you."

I had heard that voice before and I knew that it was not mine. I took my hands out of the air, stopped singing, and went forward for prayer. I told the young man, his name is Ben, who was there to pray for me how the Holy Spirit had moved me to come forward. He asked if I had any specific need and I told him, "No. God just said, 'Let him pray for you,' so go ahead and pray."

Ben started out by thanking God for my joy and asking God to empower me to take His joy to others.

He could have stopped right there. That's a tremendous prayer. But he went on to say, "God, give him direction about the calls he needs to make this week." Those words did not come from Ben. They came off of his lips, but they were spoken by the Holy Spirit.

"Okay, God," I said in my spirit. "I'll go right after the 11 o'clock service."

"Go, now."

"But there are people I—"

"Now!"

And just like George Thorogood, out the door I went.

As soon as I got in my parents' Honda Del Sol, I started praying for Joe to be alert and open to the gospel. I knew – as fully as I can know – that God was sending me to Joe. I turned on a worship CD and prayed and sung the whole twenty minute drive to the hospital.

Can I tell you that the Holy Spirit had set me on fire? Is that too much to put out there? Can the Holy Spirit still set people on fire? Will you let Him do that?

I parked the Del Sol about four blocks from the hospital (I wasn't about to drop a 5 in the hospital garage) and beat a path to Joe, just as cranked-up as the 18 year-old offensive tackle that I used to be. I would have plowed people out of the way, if necessary. By the grace of God, however, the Holy Spirit was throwing all the blocks.

I marched into that hospital, believing that God had sent me to steal a soul right out of the very clutches of satan. There may be no more powerful feeling. I told myself, "God sent me to do this and He will empower me to get it done!" I was at war and thrilled to be there. The Holy Spirit was wild within me. Yes! Yes! Yes!

I bounced off the elevator, strode tall and straight past the nurses' station, and charged my most bipolar self right boldly into Joe's room. He was dying and I was grinning from ear to ear.

Joe's wife, Yolanda, was sitting at his bedside. I would not have blamed her if she had thought I was nuts. I felt nuts. Wild, joyful, strong with the power of the Holy Spirit. There is no greater glory than knowing you are being used of God for His glory. This was all His doing. I was simply willing to go along for the ride.

Joe was awake! But his first words to me were, "Is the building on fire?!" I figured he was either way out of it or he had seen the ceiling lights flashing in the hallway. Or maybe I looked wild enough to have set the place on fire. I shook Joe's hand and told him that the building was fine.

"Good to see you," Joe said with zip. I had the impression that he was making an effort to be courteous, and I was shot through with wonder. The man was on his death bed and _he_ was concerned with making _me_ feel comfortable.

I sat beside the bed. "Joe, I heard you tried to get out of bed last night and fell on the floor."

Joe mumbled. He was not concerned about falling. He wanted to be able to walk to the bathroom and take a decent leak – just like any other man.

I crowed, "I'm surprised you were strong enough to get out of bed."

Joe wanted to be strong – physically strong. He asked Yolanda to get him a glass of water. She put it up to his lips and he griped, "Let me hold it myself." He sounded like my five-year-old nephew.

I was pleased to be speaking with Joe, but this was not about small-talk.

"How's your father?" Joe asked. A good sign.

"He's doing great. Still losing weight."

"How's Al?" Yes! Joe was lucid! Al is a friend of mine whom Joe had met a half-dozen times in the past few months at Ross Park Mall (where I am right now typing).

"Al?!" I exclaimed. "You remember Al?"

"Yeah, yeah. How is he?"

I beamed. "Ah, Joe, that's great. You remember. I thought you might be out of it."

Joe began to drift in and out of a light sleep and I knew that it was time to take the bull by the horns. I do not recall whether in that moment I asked God for help, but I knew that He was at work on it. Indeed, He had been at work on Joe for 78 years, but time was running short.

I stood up, moved close to Joe, looked in the eyes of the dying man, and fairly hollered, "Joe, I was in church this morning." He looked wide-eyed straight into my face, "Oh. You were?" he said lightly.

"Yes, I was. Somebody prayed for me and God told me to come see you."

•

Yolanda was sitting at the foot of the bed. I glanced in her direction to see if she thought I had lost my mind. I couldn't tell. What did it matter?

Joe was listening, but fading. "God loves you, Joe. And Jesus wants you to be with Him. Joe . . . Do you want to be with Jesus?"

Joe closed his eyes, nodded almost imperceptibly, and said a quiet, simple, "Yes." And fell asleep – just like he had at my last visit.

This time I was thrilled with joy. God had sent me. God empowered me. God put me in the right place at the right time and, by His grace, I spoke. And Joe said, "Yes."

Does it seem too simple? All it takes is one heartfelt and genuine "Yes" to Jesus.

It was not long after I left the hospital that I started to doubt. "Did I do it right? Should I have asked Joe if he believed that Jesus died for his sins and rose from the dead? Did I need to ask Joe if he knew he was a sinner? What about Romans 10:9? Did Joe need to confess with his mouth that Jesus is Lord?"

Those questions randomly bugged me for a few days until I talked with my brother in Christ, Mickey Burke, a no-nonsense retired City of Pittsburgh Firefighter. Mickey is boldly outspoken about his faith and every other thing that he really gives a wit about. Six years ago he told me off-the-cuff that he was going to a retreat. I said, "That sounds like something I ought to do sometime." Mickey shot back with the thumping speed of an Ali jab, "There's still room. You can come with me." My bluff had been called and I have been at Allison Park church ever since.

I told Mickey about Joe and the doubts about my witness that had been bugging me. In typical Mickey Burke fashion, he wasted no time in blasting away with what God had put on his heart and in his ever-ready mouth. "Richie, that's the enemy. God sent you there. You prayed about it and you went and did it. Don't you think the Holy Spirit was on that? If you needed to say more, the Holy Spirit would have forced the words right out of your mouth." That was good enough for me. I told Mickey about the great joy I felt when Joe said "Yes." Mickey replied and I agreed. "You would not have felt that way if you needed to say more."

That does not mean that as long as I feel good about a situation, then I can know that I did not make a mistake. My feelings can be good liars. But this situation had been bathed in prayer and surrendered to the Holy Spirit. I was committed to doing God's will. I asked for the Holy Spirit's empowerment. And I knew undeniably that witnessing to Joe was biblically commanded and that it is not God's will for any to perish. I can trust that the Holy Spirit was all over, in, and through this witness and that if I had needed to say more to Joe, the Holy Spirit, indeed, would have forced the words out of my mouth.

My friend and neighbor, today, dines with the Lord. Joe died two days after my visit. But the bipolar blessings of this episode do not end with Joe being born again and going home.

I almost missed the visitation for Joe at the funeral home. I had been told that it was scheduled for the second day after Joe's death. I learned in the afternoon of the day after he died that it was happening right now and the funeral would be tomorrow. I found that out quite by chance – or, perhaps . . . the Holy Spirit had another plan.

I quickly threw on a battleship gray suit and a hypomanic tie and hustled to the funeral home. Yolanda and her daughters (Joe's step-daughters) greeted me and we did what people do at a funeral home – make uneasy conversation while trying to figure out what we are supposed to do.

I went to the casket with Yolanda, knelt, and prayed, looking at the body of a soul who no longer needs it. A soul who is now in heaven. It still overwhelms me to realize that I know people who are right now face-to-face with Christ in the kingdom of heaven. (Barring a last minute surrender, I also know people who are right now face-to-face with an altogether contrary reality.) But that was not the further blessing that the Holy Spirit had planned.

During the visitation at the funeral home, Joe's wife and step-daughter asked me if I would like to speak at the funeral. (Do not ever offer me the chance to get up and speak in front of a group unless you mean it. I have been to law school, tried a lawsuit, seek to preach, and I have marathoner lungs. Let me speak uninterrupted to a group of people and it could be awhile before you escape.)

I truly did have a captive audience at the funeral. The congregants were squeezed into a side room and seated in rows of metal folding chairs – and I stood between them and the door. Busting out of there with some decorum was not going to be easy.

I also had a great prop/illustration for the message I was about to deliver. Joe's bones were stretched out in the box behind me, reminding my audience of their eternal destiny. And I didn't care a lick about offending anyone in that particular audience with the truth of the gospel. They had gathered for a funeral. What did they expect?

I started with a brief recitation of the standard eulogy fare. How Joe had moved into our neighborhood thirty years ago when I was a kid. How he put up with my basketball playing in the street in front of his house and never said a word about the ball going into his bushes or me tramping all over his lawn. How we could often hear him playing his trumpet even during this last bout with cancer. How when he came over do to do my parent's taxes, it would take 4 hours to do thirty minutes of returns because he and my father needed to debate their respective solutions to all of the world's problems. And then I got serious.

"Joe gave me a wonderful gift in his last days," I smiled. I was so filled with joy that I felt like I might have been glowing. "The best gift he could have given me.

"I visited Joe in the hospital this past Sunday. Yolanda was there, right by his side faithful to the end. He looked better than I expected, but we knew that he was close to the end. So, I wanted to find out how he stood with God.

"During all the time that Joe and I were neighbors, we never talked about faith, but when he got sick this last time, I did bring the subject up, but I was never really sure what he thought about God and whether he had put his faith in Christ."

At about that time, I noticed a plumply middle-aged woman with wavy-drastic, sort of blonde, long hair and ample blue make-up seated in the back row. She frowned, rolled her head from side to side, and slowly turned her eyes away from me. Perhaps the message was just for her. I imagined her to be a little angry. Strange how that motivated me.

"I did not know whether I would ever see Joe again," I pressed on. "So, I had to get down to business. I got closer to him and I started talking pretty loudly. I wanted to get his attention. I didn't want him falling asleep on me."

I repeated to the congregation what I said to Joe in the hospital.

" 'God loves you, Joe. And Jesus wants you to be with him. Joe . . . do you want to be with Jesus?' And Joe said a quiet, simple, 'Yes' and fell asleep."

I looked around at nearly every individual person in that room and smiled. One of Joe's step-daughters was crying freely.

"Joe gave me a wonderful gift in that hospital," I continued. "Because he said, 'Yes,' to Jesus, I know that right now he is in heaven with Christ. I know that might sound too simple. You just say, "Yes, Jesus, you are my Savior. I give myself to you," and you go to heaven. But, y'know, when Christ was on the Cross – being crucified – there were two thieves hanging there with Him. One of them mocked Christ and said, 'If you really are the Son of God, then why don't you bring yourself down off that Cross and take us down, too?' And the other thief said, 'Have you no fear of God even now when you are about to die? We deserve to be here, but this man has done no wrong.' And that thief turned to Jesus and said, 'Jesus, remember me when you come into your kingdom.'"

"I know this might sound too simple," I said to the small congregation, "but Jesus did not say to that thief, 'You gotta be kidding. Man, you've got some real guts. All your life you're a sinner and a thief and now you come, at the last minute, begging to get into heaven.' Jesus did not say that. He looked at the thief on the cross and, as the thief was dying, he said, "I assure you, this day, you will be with me in paradise."'

I looked around the room one more time, smiling into as many eyes as I could, "Joe gave me a wonderful gift . . . right there in that hospital. . . He said, 'Yes,' to Jesus. And, because of that, I know, this day, Joe is with Jesus in paradise."

When the Holy Sprit pushed me forward and demanded that I go to Ben for prayer at the end of the 11 o'clock service at Allison Park Church, I had no idea what he had in store for me. Thank God, the Holy Spirit kept pushing. Because of Him, I got to comfort Joe with the same comfort I was given by a recovering alcoholic twenty years earlier in a psych hospital just down the road from the hospital in which Joe died. I saw Joe accept Christ just two days before his death. And I got to witness to a captive audience which included that middle-aged woman with the wavy-drastic, sort of blonde, long hair and ample blue make-up.

"God whispers to us in our pleasures, speaks in our consciences,

but shouts in our pains: it is His megaphone to rouse a deaf world."

- C.S. Lewis

CHAPTER 19

THE CRAZINESS OF CHRISTIANITY

Occasionally, in the midst of a church service, I realize that the most crucial matter in my life is sheer absurdity in the eyes of non-Christians. (1Corinthians 1:18, 21b, 23, 25, 27; 2:14) But, because I have bipolar disorder, I am comfortably acquainted with that look staring back at me that says, "Oh, yeah, this guy's got a screw loose." It has given me the chance to understand the uneasiness, curiosity, amusement, and even anger that a person may feel when they encounter something that, in their experience, looks and sounds bizarre. And, because I have bipolar disorder, there have been times when seeing that look in another's face did *not* inhibit my madness. So, I was blessed with the full measure of how people deal with me as a perceived whack-job. It was frustrating at first, but I eventually concluded that they just don't 'get it.' They do not know the blessings of bipolar disorder. (Could it be that this book is written for them?)

And non-believers who think that Christians are nuts – just don't 'get it.' That does not offend me. They cannot comprehend the strength, joy, wonder, victory, and love that we know in, through, and with Christ. They do not have the Spirit of all truth living within them, opening the scriptures to their minds, and revealing Christ.

If we believers are to have any Godly impact upon the beliefs of non-Christians, then we must understand their perspective and not be offended by their doubts about our connection with reality.

If a Chicago Cubs fan comes at me and says, "Your Pirates are the dung heap of the Major Leagues, the road to baseball hell," he will have no chance of convincing me that the Cubs are a serious contender. He may have rock-solid arguments backed with irrefutable SABRmetric calculations, but his witness will instantly fail if he starts with an outright blasting of my undying support for the Pirates. I just will not listen. In fact, I would probably mention the 63 years since his Cubs last appeared in a World Series. (p.s. They lost.)

It is the same with my attempts to persuade those who have a caricatured understanding of bipolar disorder that it can be a blessing rather than a reason to swiftly abandon my presence.

Many people whose knowledge of bipolar disorder comes entirely from tabloid TV (that may not include all nightly news broadcasts) have some not so realistic fears of people like me. They think we are all permanently on the verge of a raging mood swing, threatening bloodshed. I cannot change their minds by telling them that they don't know what they are talking about. I have to acknowledge the piece of truth in their fearful understanding. There are times when I do have raging mood swings. And I have lost my temper to the point of "physical confrontation." When I calmly acknowledge my less endearing symptoms, the other person knows that I understand where they are coming from. Only then can they open up to the possibility that there may be something more to me than a fistful of mania. After all, I haven't smacked the snot out of them for assuming that I am perpetually violent.

The same is true of our efforts to bring Christ to the non-Christian. If I do not start with a respectful understanding of their unbelief, they are not going to respect my belief or my efforts to show them what they are missing. And the more zealously I try, the more likely they are to attempt an escape.

I can't go at a non-Christian and start a witness by saying – even in a nice-guy-squishy-couldn't-hurt-a-fly voice – "Y'know, I'm sorry, but there is really no doubt that Jesus is the Savior of the world and the only way to heaven. I mean, He died on the cross and rose from the dead to pay for your sin . . . Please, don't get me wrong. I'm sorry. I don't mean to offend you, but that's not coming from me. That's the Bible."

I may have the purest of intentions – the eternal salvation of the unbeliever's soul. But in one-half of my first sentence I have shut the ears, closed the mind, and hardened the heart of my friendly non-Christian acquaintance.

When I open up with, "There is no doubt that Jesus —," I have already thrown the unbeliever on the defensive. I have immediately disregarded and denied his perspective and his God-given right to have his own "doubt that Jesus —." God granted him a will that is just as free as mine and he has, thus far, chosen to use that will to not believe. I disagree with him, but I must respect his right to be so deadly wrong – if I hope to have any chance of helping him to see the truth.

Put yourself in the shoes of the unbeliever for a minute. Imagine that you only believe what you can see, hear, touch, and/or taste. If you cannot perceive it with your senses or prove it through the scientific method, then it isn't real. You have been convinced of this attitude since childhood and have never had any reason to doubt it. The question never enters your mind. From that perspective what would you think of somebody telling you not only that there is a reality outside of what you perceive with your physical senses, but insisting that unseen reality is the one essential fact of all existence? And that unless you agree with him, you won't just die; you will die and suffer eternal torture after your death? What would you think of that person? How about, "Nutcase?" The notion *'bipolar'* might even cross your mind. I know whereof I speak. I have seen people look at me and think, "Nutcase," with facts to support their finding.

We who have been convinced by the power of the Holy Spirit that Jesus is the Son of God; lived a perfect life; died to pay the penalty for our sins; *rose from the dead*(!); ascended into heaven; and is coming back any day now to claim His kingdom, sometimes forget just how extraordinarily out of touch with reality that sounds to one who is in the world *and* of the world. To the unbeliever it sounds like me screaming with a 6-foot-4-inch, red-faced, and white-hot glare, "Bipolar is a (cuss) blessing!" My passion defeats my argument by looking crazy and flat-out denying the other person's previous understanding and experience. And I drive them away.

Yes, we must be passionate about witnessing of Christ and the absolute, eternal truth of the Good News. But we have to keep in mind that the goal is not to demand that people see things our way, but to bring them to Christ. We are not trying to win arguments, but souls. And if our unbelieving friends do put their faith in Jesus, they will *not* see Him the way you or I do. In fact, you and I do not see Him in the same way. Does Jesus not have a unique relationship with each one of us?

If I want to convince a person of the blessings of bipolar disorder, I must first acknowledge their experience of it as a dreadful, dangerous, and agonizing curse. If I want to have any hope of bringing an atheist to Christ, I must first be understanding of the fact that he lives in a world that has so much trouble with the man we call Lord that it nailed Him to a tree and killed Him. It may not be so easy to go quickly from that perspective to one of absolute surrender. And I am sure to look crazy trying to convince him. But I have looked crazy before – and with far less motivation.

"Let people feel the weight of who you are and let them deal with it."
- John Eldredge (2001, p.149)

CHAPTER 20

RESEARCH STUDIES

If you have bipolar disorder, your brain does not work like the garden variety "normal" brain. It is unique, unlike 99% of the rest of the world's brains. That makes your brain interesting. Science has much yet to learn about what goes on inside your head – and mine. That gives us the opportunity to be involved in research that will teach us more about our bipolar brains and how to use our disorder more effectively.

How many times have you heard that bipolar disorder is a "chemical imbalance" in the brain? Over and again? Even before you were diagnosed? I have heard those words repeatedly, especially when others were trying to convince me that bipolar disorder is a physical illness that requires treatment not just of our thoughts and emotions, but of the body. (medication to treat the neurological processes of the brain.)

Eventually I accepted the evidence that bipolar is, at least in part, related to a chemical imbalance in the brain. But, in 20 years of treatment, I have never been told which chemicals are out of balance and what are the optimal levels of those chemicals, and how they are supposed to function. I don't think anyone really knows (other than serotonin's effect on depression).

There is something out of the ordinary going on in the bipolar brain. But nobody seems to know precisely what processes and chemicals are out of whack. Or how to get them in whack.

The lack of understanding of the bipolar brain is a source of frustration. We struggle and cause others pain without an explanation. But there are people who are working to find out what is happening in our brains and what actions we can take to bring our thoughts, emotions, and behaviors more under our control.

I do not want my brain and its processes to be completely explained and understood. I do not want a neuro-chemical brain formula to coldly calculate why I love somebody or have faith or think abstractly and have better language skills than arithmetic abilities. In fact, I don't believe that such a precise formula is possible. It does not exist to be found – in my unscientific, but thoroughly lived opinion.

I do not believe that science will ever be able to determine or "create" an individual's personality by figuring out – or manipulating – the physical actions and reactions going on in the brain. I insist on my God-given free will. (Even my misbegotten, fool-hearty, and dangerous bipolar decisions are my own free will decisions.) But I do want science to learn what is going on in our bipolar brains when we struggle with our thinking, emotions, physiology, and behavior.

Because I want medical science to learn what chemicals and neurological processes are out of whack during a bipolar episode, I am willing and eager to participate in research studies that seek to understand bipolar disorder. Our bipolar brains *are* unique and, therefore, highly interesting. They are an experience that others cannot know – and that experience gives us something to offer medical science.

We are the experts on our own lived experience of how our unique bipolar brains impact our thinking, feeling, and acting. As such, we are an irreplaceable and necessary asset to medical researchers. Without us, they cannot learn much about bipolar. We are a blessing to them and to those who will come after us who will be blessed with bipolar.

I participated last week – as a bipolar subject - in a study that is examining the interaction between psychiatrists and their patients who have bipolar disorder. I do not know precisely what the study is seeking to learn, but I want to do what I can to advance the knowledge regarding the disorder. I want people with bipolar disorder to succeed to the fullest of their massive potential, beyond what they believe they are capable of achieving.

I do not participate in research studies because I want bipolar to be cured. I participate because I believe bipolar is a misunderstood blessing. Blessings don't need a cure. I want the blessing of bipolar to be better understood so that those of us who are so blessed can use it to succeed, to prosper, to use our uniquely gifted brains to do great things for ourselves, our families, our God, and society. I want us to be able to harness (not stop!) our tremendous and enviable bipolar energy for good.

I have wondered what my life would be like if I did not have bipolar or if there were a cure that I could have taken at an early age.

I imagine myself staying at Georgia Tech, becoming one of their starting offensive tackles or guards, getting well-connected in the Atlanta community, and not having a school loan to repay.

I imagine being able to keep a good job and succeeding professionally and financially.

I imagine marrying a gifted, beautiful, and intelligent, Christian woman who is strong enough to stand up to me; unburdened by bipolar disruptions to our life together. I think of us raising wonderful, talented, tough, God-fearing, motivated renaissance children with many and varied interests. ("Well-rounded," their Grandma Lucy would say.)

I imagine not losing my law school scholarship, representing students and families, standing up to the incompetencies, waste, and unconcern of our public (government) school system. And not having that St. Thomas University School of Law loan to repay.

Indeed, there are times when I believe that if not for bipolar disorder, the 2008 republican presidential ticket would have been McCain - Ya'Zhynka. (You laugh? I am a 46 year-old conservative from blue-state Pennsylvania, who was raised a Catholic, played college football in Georgia, worked 15 years with troubled youth, is pro-life, and attends an Assembly of God church. That covers a swing-state, Catholics, evangelicals, younger voters, and everyone who is concerned about "the children." And without bipolar disorder there would not be that **false** allegation of threatening to blow-up St. Thomas University's legal writing lab to deal with. I'd be the perfect compliment to John McCain. Remember, I'm allowed delusions of grandeur – as long as I don't believe I am the nominee, go out raising money, campaigning, and stalking the senator, believing that I have been nominated.)

On the other hand, I also wonder whether without bipolar disorder I would have had the mental and physical energy and desire to accomplish any of the things that I *have* done. Would I have been able to summon the intense energy I needed to workout and become strong enough to play scholarship-level football? Would I have had the passion to take the field and so wildly slam my body as hard as I could into other bodies? Would I have had whatever madness it is that convinces one that pain matters less than finishing 26.2 miles of a marathon? Would *not* having bipolar disorder have meant a loss of IQ? Would my thoughts processes have been changed to the point where my mental aptitudes would not have been inclined toward law and psychology? Without depression, failure, anxiety, rage, guilt, and despair would I have felt my sin enough to know that I need a Savior?

I choose not to dwell on what I might or *might not* have accomplished without bipolar disorder and to embrace the fact that I have achieved goals with the help of bipolar disorder.

Bipolar does not define my very being. It is not my identity. But it does impact my personality and influence my thoughts, world-view, emotions, and interpretations of events and ideas.

I have never _not_ had bipolar disorder, so, I do not know quite what I would be like without it. And I am not so interested in knowing. I do not want science to teach me what I might have achieved without bipolar disorder. I want scientific research to teach me and others how to achieve more than we ever imagined possible – by using the unique blessings of bipolar disorder!

I want science to better learn how the bipolar brain works so it can be an even greater blessing. Who knows? Maybe someday they'll cut mine right out of its skull and have a good look at it.

*"Happiness depends on happenings
But joy depends on Christ."*

- unknown author
(quoted at ChristianMingle.com)

CHAPTER 21

THIS TOO SHALL PASS

A bomb exploded in the middle of my life when I was expelled from St. Thomas University School of Law. I was hurt, angry and confused. And fighting the lawsuit against the school without an attorney became my life's work for over four years.[2]

I wish I did not have to admit this because it is not good for Christians – or anyone else for that matter – to be consumed with anything but Christ. But there were times when I was consumed with the lawsuit and expulsion. Now, not two years later, thank God, I can hardly get interested in it enough to write about it. It just doesn't seem to matter anymore beyond the specific circumstances that I mention here as examples of the blessings of bipolar.

However...I have had this nagging sense of being obligated to put the thing down on paper in detail. But I have not been able to bring myself to sit down and tell the full story beginning to end. That puzzles me. It seems worthy of at least a chapter. In fact, I had thought I would write a book about it. That was my plan prior to almost accidentally starting this book.

The expulsion/lawsuit deal seems like a good tale to tell. My guess is that it doesn't happen to most people. Add in the fact that I was falsely accused of wanting to blow up a building and being "on a divine mission to save the soul" of a professor and it would seem to get even more interesting. And a bipolar man representing himself in federal court without a law degree…well, now that just has to be a story, screwy enough to publish.[2]

So, why have I not been able to tell the tale? Why haven't I been able to recount the events that swept me out-of-the-blue from Pittsburgh to Miami, pitted me snarling face-to-face with a law professor in a men's room, commanded me into exile, and landed me before the Eleventh Circuit Federal Court of Appeals?

Answer: I cannot write out the details start to finish because it honestly just does not interest me all that much anymore. And that fact is the very reason for this chapter: No matter, how overwhelming, all-consuming, and just plain bad the present moment may be – This Too Shall Pass.

One of the things that can make bipolar depressive episodes so dreadful to endure is that in that moment one can have the distorted belief that it will never end. It isn't true. The episode always ends. It may take a while and in the midst of the episode it may seem like things have always been miserable, but it will end.

(There are, or course, some life-changing tragedies that are so severe and cause such unavoidable emotional trauma that it would be foolish of me to argue that the pain will ever fully go away. But we can get to the point where it is not so all-consuming and we are free to move into the rest of our life.)

The expulsion/lawsuit was an epic battle that I fought with passion, perseverance, love, and anger. It forced me to continue studying the law, to read hundreds upon hundreds of cases, to write numerous arguments that I would have called impossible before I filed the initial complaint. I was absorbed with it for five-and-a-half years. I raved with mad enthusiasm over it. I barked at my opponents. I straight-faced my way through a mediation conference in which I exposed – with documentation – the lie of an opposing attorney seated directly across the table from me. I had my faith maligned and stood up for it. I was inspired and punched my fists in the air, confident of victory and certain that my God was with me. I was broken and punched my fists in the air, growling, "My God, why have you abandoned me?" It was an amazing, extreme experience that helped to change me and lead me closer to God in ways that I write about in other chapters of this book. But the details just don't seem to matter much anymore. This too has passed.

The expulsion and lawsuit became so desperately important to me that I falsely believed that my future success or failure depended entirely upon winning the lawsuit. There were many times when I was not sure how I would go on if I lost. Times of such despair that I failed to function for days. I Was Wrong.

I lost and the world did not end. The desperation passed. And life is now better than ever. I could not possibly have believed that things could be so good after losing that lawsuit.

Learning that I did not need to win may well be a greater blessing than actually winning would have been. (*I might feel otherwise if a jury had awarded me all of the damages I was asking for. It was no small sum. Nah. It would have ruined me. Maybe. Alright, so, I wouldn't have minded finding out. You can't sue me for that.*)

I want you to be reassured. You may not see it, but I know you can imagine the light at the end of the tunnel. It is there!

No matter how desperate your current circumstances may be (and I have no doubt that there is legitimate reason for unavoidable pain), no matter the depth of agitated depression you may now be struggling, no matter the extreme bipolar episode, financial failure, or relationship breakdown – This Too Shall Pass. There can and will come a day when this dire moment is over. Hang on! God really is at work. He is for you and not against you. He *is* with you. His strength *is*, *indeed*, made perfect in your weakness. Hang on! THIS TOO SHALL PASS.

I've been there.

(In Jesus' Name)
I tear down the stronghold of DEPRESSION.
The joy of the Lord will be our strength.

I shake off the spirit of heaviness
and put on the garment of praise.

I shake off the spirit of heaviness
and put on the garment of praise.

I shake off the atmosphere of depression . . .

I declare a breakthrough
in the heavenly realms.
My life will be marked with praise
and with joy.

- Chris Griffin and Jeff Leake,
Allison Park Church Pastors

CHAPTER 22

SOCIAL SECURITY DISABILITY INCOME

Some would describe me as a free-loader, deadbeat, bum leach. A drain on society. Why? Because I receive social security disability income (SSDI) as a result of having bipolar disorder.

Allow me to ask the above-mentioned skeptics whether they would hire me after learning during their search process that I was hospitalized seven times for bipolar disorder, lost numerous jobs because of agitated manic-depressive episodes, and was expelled from law school on the very day that the Dean learned that I have bipolar disorder. To those who say that I should get off my dead behind, get a job, and go to work, I say, "Hire me. I dare ya!"

I had bipolar disorder prior to the day in 1976 when I started a summer job at the paint manufacturing company where my father worked in Pittsburgh's Strip District. I was 14.

I struggled with major depression and mania during the semesters when I worked two jobs (part-time lifeguard and full-time child care worker in a residential treatment facility for court-adjudicated kids) while taking three undergraduate courses at Duquesne University.

I lived with bipolar disorder, untreated, while I worked in a school and partial-hospital classroom with violent, inner-city teenagers.

I had bipolar disorder when I was spit on, cursed, kicked, and punched – all in the course of doing my job.

I lost social service jobs due to bipolar disorder when I got too depressed to continue or finally blew my stack – after willingly going into chaotic, disturbed, and abusive home situations that one would do anything to avoid in one's own family. And I kept on applying for new jobs and going back to work, never giving the slightest consideration to applying for Social Security Disability Income (SSDI).

I was first hospitalized for my bipolar disorder in 1988 – for two months. Upon my discharge, I gave no consideration to applying for SSDI.

Over the next 18 years I held at least 14 different jobs with 14 different organizations. I was hospitalized six more times.

In July 1999 I was fired from a job as Director of a family counseling program. I had testified on behalf of a family who was attempting to have their children returned from the custody of the county's Department of Children and Youth Services (CYS). CYS vehemently opposed the family. The judge agreed with my recommendation – against the wishes of CYS. The same CYS, that is, which funded our program. I was fired 11 days later.

After being fired as Program Director, rather than considering SSDI, I attempted to change fields. I went to law school at the age of 38. That's a drastic change of life for a man approaching middle-age. But I did it in the hope of being productive, supporting myself, and making a contribution rather than applying for disability. I wanted to work and be financially responsible.

After I was expelled from law school within one day of the Dean learning of my disorder, I went back to work as a counselor.[1] I was fired from that job after confronting an ex-con father regarding his mistreatment of his autistic son. I admit that I also had trouble keeping up with the paper work. The job and the stress of trying my lawsuit was causing bipolar to mess with me. But I still did not consider SSDI.

My point in all of this is that I did not leap at the chance to leave the workforce and collect a government check. From the time I was first hospitalized in 1988, it took 18 years, 14 jobs, 6 more hospitalizations, a plethora of psychotropic medications, an expulsion from law school, and the loss of my lawsuit before I finally applied for SSDI.

If you think I should go back to work, hire me. I dare ya!

SSDI is not welfare. I paid into it nearly every hour that I worked (part-time, full-time, or summers) from 1976 until 2003. I could have applied the first time I cracked-up in 1988. But I held onto the hope of being able to work and succeed until I finally lost my lawsuit in December 2006. I could no longer beat my head against that wall. When the federal court system failed me, I decided to take the safety net that I had paid into. And I thank God that I live in a country that has the compassion to provide such a program to people who are too handicapped to remain in the workforce.

Some people will say that there surely must be some work that I can do. "He's written a book," they will argue, "Doesn't that prove that he shouldn't be on disability?"

I do not deny that there is work that I can do – when I am not too manic or depressed and if I can do it when I want to do it, the way I want to do it, and without a boss dragging over my shoulder. I never know when I will or will not be able to function. (I write because I can do it only when and if I feel like doing it. There is nobody making demands about how and when it gets done. Therefore, if I do not feel like writing, then it does not need to get done.)

Being forced to be at a specific job, for a specific 40 hours per week, doing things according to somebody else's directions would, in short order, cause me to blow a fuse. Or, as the vocational expert at my disability hearing said, "<u>He is incapable of interacting in a socially appropriate manner</u>." Bipolar can do that. There is documentation. But that does not mean that I am out of control 24 hours a day. Just that bipolar prevents me from continuously interacting in a way necessary to maintaining regular employment.

Do you know of any companies that would allow me to have as many sick days as necessary, that I could take whenever necessary, on the spur of the moment, and possibly for a month at a time?

If being on SSDI helps to keep me sane enough to stay out of the psych ward, then my benefits may actually be saving the government some money. A thirty day hospital stay could amount to as much money as I will receive on SSDI in three years – maybe more.

I am a political conservative. I believe in small government, low taxes, cutting Washington's wasteful spending, financial responsibility, free market capitalism, the right to life, a strong national defense, and the sovereignty of the fifty individual states. But Social Security Disability is a legitimate and necessary government program. There are citizens of this country who truly cannot work due to a handicap. And once they have gone through the thorough and rigorous governmental process of determining that they are no longer medically capable of working, the government must provide a safety net.

We who receive SSDI have either paid into the program or have been severely handicapped all of our lives. We did not choose to be medically incapable of being a part of the workforce.

If bipolar disorder has caused you to be unable to work for significant periods of time or repeatedly interrupted your ability to work, I urge you to look into social security disability income. Knowing that you have a financial safety net may relieve some of the work-related stress that can sometimes exacerbate your symptoms. There is no shame in receiving SSDI and receiving it does *not* mean that you can never work again. In fact, once a person is awarded SSDI, he is permitted to earn a specific, though small, monthly sum of money and still receive benefits. Also, if your condition improves and you attempt to return to full-time employment, social security will continue to pay your full monthly benefits for your first nine months of work. (Social Security Administration, January 2009, Publication No. 05-10095)

Rather than reporting to a full-time job every morning, I now spend my time writing at Ross Park Mall (Yeah, that sounds strange. Consider it bipolar); researching and reading everything that catches my interest; singing in the choir, the car; and the shower; studying the Pittsburgh Pirates; swimming; lifting weights; cross-training and climbing. I can do these things in spite of bipolar disorder because I can do them when I want to, how I want to, and without a boss scrounging over my shoulder. And I can choose not to do them whenever bipolar rears up – without the risk of getting fired or expelled. Of course, these activities and all of my life are a bit easier without the pressure of being obligated to a job while roiling with bipolar.

It was not my choice to have a handicap and applying for SSDI was a last resort after 18 years of drastically mood disordered employment. I know that I have made long, sincere, and repeated effort to gain and hold employment. For those reasons, I will receive SSDI as long as necessary, without shame. However, I hope that I will someday be able to, at least partially, support myself through writing, preaching, and private practice counseling – whenever I may be medically capable.

I won't be able to write, preach, or counsel as a full-time, or even part-time, employee, but if I can do it on my own, whenever capable, with the freedom to not do it whenever not capable, then I have the hope of being productive. Knowing that there is a safety net if bipolar causes me to fall, I believe that it is possible for me to be productive.

Again, I thank God that I live in a country where the taxpayers are willing to compassionately support SSDI. It is a blessing.

The cords of death entangled me,
*   the anguish of the grave came*
*   upon me;*
I was overcome by trouble and
*   sorrow.*
Then I called on the name of the
*   Lord:*
*   "O Lord, save me!"*

The Lord is gracious and righteous;
*   our God is full of compassion.*
The Lord protects the
*   simplehearted;*
When I was in great need, he
*   saved me.*

Be at rest once more, O my soul,
*   for the Lord has been good to*
*   you.*

For you, O Lord, have delivered
*   my soul from death,*
*   my eyes from tears,*
*   my feet from stumbling,*
that I may walk before the Lord
*   in the land of the living.*

Psalm 116:3-9

CHAPTER 23

IMPULSIVITY

|CAUTION: *Impulsivity is obviously not always a blessing and I do not mean to make light of the serious harm that it can cause. A person who has bipolar disorder is sometimes prone to an impulsivity that can lead to dangerous, unwise, and destructive actions. This symptom must be taken seriously. My intention with this chapter is to demonstrate that the impulsivity of bipolar can inspire creativity and motivate positive action. However, this impulsivity, when not harnessed with sound judgment and the wise counsel of real friends, can also lead to extreme risk-taking behaviors resulting in serious injury. (Remember, I'm the man who had the loony impulse to kick a punching bag and ended up with his leg in a boot for six weeks) This symptom must be taken seriously in order to* *keep safe the person who has bipolar and those around him.*]

It is June 8, 2008 and I am sitting in the food court at Ross Park Mall with my own nearly empty head. But I just had an inspiration light up my brain and say, "Pull out your notebook. Pick up that blue Fodi's Tavern pen and write."

"C'mon," I moan, "can't I shut it down awhile – give my head a break and just stop thinkin' for a minute - or sixty."

But the green light keeps flashing: "Go ahead. Just keep your hand moving that pen across the page. How long can that bipolar brain keep firing something out that might be worth getting down on paper."

"Oh, yeah. Yeah! As I was driving here I was thinking about faith and how living without it is suicidal." Bang! And the hand moves.

Everybody has faith. Well, not everybody. Those who have no faith are curled up in a catatonic ball, terrified to face the world in even the slightest and safest degree. And it makes some sense to do so. This world is a dangerous place. Abundant threats abound. Things do go wrong. People do get hurt. Automobile collisions happen to the most considerate and safest of drivers. You can look both ways and still get plowed daring to leave the curb. At any given moment disaster could strike and often does.

My sisters' apartment burned to the ground through no fault of their own. They were out on a Saturday afternoon trip to a Nashville shopping mall with my three year-old nephew while his father – my brother-in-law – was at work. The wiring in a wall of my nephew's bedroom went bad and started an electrical fire. They never went home to that apartment again. In an instant, their earthly home no longer existed. They lost almost all of their possessions. They did nothing to cause the fire. Nothing. And yet they had no home to return to from their playful Saturday afternoon trip to the mall.

Bad things do happen. Sometimes, out of nowhere and without the least warning. Curling up in a terrified, catatonic ball – mentally, physically, and emotionally shutting down for one's own preservation – does make some sense.

"So," I ask, "Why don't we all curl up?"

And I hear you say, "Idiot. Who wants to live like that?"

Exactly.

The vast majority of people do not live in Catatonia. What, then, moves us beyond that level of maximum self-preservation, protection, and safety in an inherently dangerous world?

No sooner are we conceived than we are in danger of ceasing to exist. How do we step into that danger and put ourselves at still greater risk of ceasing to exist – a risk that most of us take every day? What does it take to do that?

Faith.

When you walk through a crosswalk, you place your faith in every stranger behind the wheel of a thousand pound vehicle approaching that intersection. You believe that they will stop. You cannot be sure that they will. And yet you're not still standing on that corner. You unconsciously trust that strange, unknown driver to follow the rules of the road – and that he is actually paying attention, is halfway sober, and sees the red light. _That_ is faith.

The psychologist Erik Erikson set forth a theory of human psychological development which consisted of a series of conflicts at every stage of development. (Erickson, 1963, pp.247-274) Healthy development requires some degree of successful resolution of each conflict.

Erickson names the conflict faced in the first and most essential stage "Basic Trust versus Basic Mistrust." (p.247-251) In order to move on, the individual at this stage of development must come to some way of trusting that this dangerous world will not completely destroy him/her. The alternatives can be severe: catatonia, failure to thrive, infant death, schizophrenia. Most of us succeed at partially resolving this conflict. Anger, fear, and anxiety, however, are issues that have their genesis in this first stage of development.

Duquesne University psychology professor Richard Knowles theorizes that in resolving each Ericksonian conflict the individual develops a virtue or strength. (1986, p.17) He identifies 'hope' as the virtue of the first stage of development and the "most fundamental or basic strength to be considered." (1986, pp.21-22) I would call the same virtue 'faith.' The infant overcomes the dilemma of being hurled without his/her consent into a troubled and dangerous world by putting his/her faith (hope or trust) in its parents. When there is no adult in whom that infant trusts there is a developmental crisis to which the infant may respond with severe disturbance. (1986, p.27)

But even the best parents cannot be ever-present and perfect safe-guards one-hundred percent of the time. And the world is still a dangerous place. We need somebody we can count on completely, in every situation, all of the time. Most of us spend a lot of time trying to convince ourselves that we are that person. "I can take care of myself," we boldly proclaim. Bob Dylan (1985) sings, I hope sarcastically, "If you want somebody you can trust, trust yourself." Most of us keep trying to do that no matter how many times we fall flat on our faces. And we are doomed to fail.

We are not secure. The world is not safe. It cannot be trusted. People do damage to each other. Natural disasters happen. And we don't have what it takes to get ourselves through emotionally unscathed. Contrary to what my favorite singer/songwriter/philosopher says above, if you want somebody you can trust . . . "it ain't you, babe."

It ain't science, either. Or medicine, art, philosophy, psychology, law, or religion. (Science once said that the flat earth was the center of the universe. And religious ritual without faith is no better than superstition.) They help give some order to the way we are living and they are, at times, a comfort, but they all fall short. They change. They make mistakes. They are shifting sand. Build your life on them and you will be washed away.

We are insecure creations in an ever-changing world. Our very desire for security means insecurity.

(Watts, 1951, pp.77-78) And what is this security for which we search? How do we get it? Trust. Just like the infant, we need to know that somebody will protect us in this world full of threats. We need to know that somebody loves us perfectly. That there is somebody we can trust completely all of the time. A perfect parent. A perfect Father. God.

Security means stability, permanence, unchanging certainty. Is there anything in all creation that can provide that? Trust yourself? You're changing all the time. How much can you really control? Your life moves continuously, influenced by people and events outside of your awareness. It's not your fault. It's the condition of the world. You are not the person you were one year ago. The people close to you are not who they were a year ago. A day ago.

What is stable, permanent, unchanging, and certain? Only God Eternal. Only in Him can we find our security because only He is the same yesterday, today, and tomorrow. (Hebrews 13:8)

We all put faith in something. We know very little with certainty. "I experience, therefore, I exist." (My existential-phenomenological paraphrase of Descartes) That's about all I really know. Everything else comes down to faith. And faith is nothing other than choosing to believe something in spite of the doubts I have about it. Yes, even faith in God means choosing to believe something I cannot know for sure. But faith in anything other than God means trusting in something that I have experienced to be insecure, passing, and just about as unreliable as I know myself to be.

You may not believe in God, but you cannot deny that you have faith. You could not get out of bed without it. You would be catatonic. You believe in something or someone that you cannot prove. It may be family or friends. (We all must have some reasonable amount of trust in people. Otherwise, relationship would be impossible.) It may be work, success, money, power, and/or fame. It may be karma, the magic of the cosmos, astrology, or the alleged fairness of the universe. But it is faith that enables you to function in this world that is a constant threat to your very existence. Faith in something or someone you believe will endure – even when _you_ don't.

And I would not have written any of this section had it not been for the symptom of bipolar impulsivity which stirred through my head and buzzed, "Write something, anything. Just keep your hand moving."

> [**CAUTION:** *Impulsivity is obviously not always a blessing and I do not mean to make light of the serious harm that it can cause. A person who has bipolar disorder is sometimes prone to an impulsivity that can lead to dangerous, unwise, and destructive actions. This symptom must be taken seriously. My intention with this chapter is to demonstrate that the impulsivity of bipolar can inspire creativity and motivate positive action. However, this impulsivity, when not harnessed with sound judgment and the wise counsel of real friends, can also lead to extreme risk-*

taking behaviors resulting in serious injury. (Remember, I'm the man who had the loony impulse to kick a punching bag and ended up with his leg in a boot for six weeks) This symptom must be taken seriously in order to keep safe the person who has bipolar and those around him.]

*"When you set yourself on fire,
people love to come and watch you burn."*
- John Wesley

CHAPTER 24

GOD, GAYS, AND A GOOFBALL'S BRAIN

Hold it against me if you like, but I watch FOX News – CNN, too, and, if I'm feeling especially brave-hearted, MSNBC. I know that as an American male I am supposed to be stereotypically consumed with ESPN, beer, and the female anatomy, but at least two of those three can be deadly for me. The other merely kills brain cells.

I often find politics more interesting than sports. It's the same level of combat, but it actually has real-life consequences. (No, the Super Bowl only has real-life consequences if you wager the mortgage. In which case, there are more pressing neuroses to address than *either* sports *or* politics.) So, forgive me, I watch FOX News.

Last night, my favorite cable news outlet, played video of a group of homosexuals protesting outside of Saddleback Church in California. Rick Warren, the well-known pastor of the church and author of <u>The Purpose-Driven Life</u> (2002), had supported proposition 8 – a referendum to ban gay marriage which was passed by the people of California in the election of November 4, 2008.

The protest by homosexuals got me to thinking about the appropriate response of a Christian to a person who is gay.

Two biblical teachings quickly sprang to mind. First, the Bible does clearly state that homosexual behavior is a sin. Second, the Bible clearly states that those who claim to follow Christ are to love all people. That "*all*" would seem to include people who commit homosexual sin.

I have a unique perspective on the issue because I did not choose to have bipolar disorder, just as homosexuals claim that they did not choose to be gay, but rather were born with a genetic pre-determination for same-sex attraction.

Some Christians claim that God would not create a person as a homosexual. I am not going to make that argument. Instead, I am asking the question, "What if God did allow a person to be born with a genetic pre-disposition toward same-sex attraction?"

My first thought, upon asking myself this question, was that it would seem unfair for God to create a person with a pre-disposition toward a behavior that he clearly calls sin. Would that not mean that God had contradicted Himself? And, don't we, as Christians, believe that it is impossible for God to contradict Himself since He is all-perfect-truth and eternally consistent wisdom – the same yesterday, today, and tomorrow? If that is so, then how could such a God at one moment call homosexuality sin and at another moment create people genetically pre-disposed to commit that very sin?

Doesn't it seem unfair and even cruel, especially for a supposedly all-loving God, to author such conflict between what He expects from a person and how He creates that person?

Therefore, I can understand why Christians would want to resolve this dilemma by contending that God would never create somebody as a homosexual and that people who are gay choose same-sex attraction.

(When I speak of 'choice,' in this sense, I am not limiting it to a deliberate and thorough pre-mediation. There are choices that we only realize as such reflectively, after we have made them. For instance, when I leave a room I may simply get up and go without any thought. But when I look back on the experience I would certainly not deny that I willingly chose to get up and leave the room.)

On the other hand, I can also understand why a person who is gay would claim that "they were born that way," and, therefore, homosexuality cannot be a sin. I would imagine that it does not feel like one chooses same-sex attraction. I have never felt like I had to choose to find attractive the female anatomy (regardless of whether it is deadly for me or merely kills brain cells).

However, my second thought on the issue is that I was born with a genetically pre-disposed and chemically imbalanced bipolar brain. And my God-given brain results in volatile mood swings that sometimes include ferocious anger. Just like the homosexual, I believe that I was "born that way" – that I did not choose to have a bipolar brain. (Although, in retrospect, if given the choice, I may now opt for it. Hence, the book.)

So, another question arises. Since I was born with a bipolar brain and a genetic propensity toward ferocious anger, is it a sin for me to pick a fight and kick somebody's ass? If I was born that way, isn't it unfair for God to expect me not to kick ass? Well, he might not expect me to win, but wouldn't it still be unfair for Him to expect me not to start fist-fights even if it's my butt that turns up on the kicked end?

A quick review of my scripture-memory makes me vaguely sense that God does not think it unfair to create me with bipolar disorder and still expect me not to go angrily looking to start a brawl. In fact, He says, "[B]e quick to listen, slow to speak, and slow to become angry." (James 1:19) And, "In your anger do not sin." (Ephesians 4:26)There is also something in there about cheeks and being struck (Matthew 5:39) that He hasn't finished working on me with, yet.

What stands out to me in those verses is that God does not say, "Thou shalt never get angry." The verses, indeed, acknowledge that we certainly will get angry.

So, this is my dilemma:

1. God has created me with a bipolar brain.
2. My bipolar brain has a predisposition toward ferocious anger.

3. God says it is a sin for me to start a fist-fight – even when my God-given brain throws a mood-swing complete with ferocious anger in the presence of some creature who keenly deserves to be battered about the skull.

Does this make God unfair? He created me this way and yet He will not accept my acting on it. In fact, He says that the consequence of acting out my genetic pre-disposition is hell. [The wages of sin being death eternal. (Romans 6:23)]

But my condition and God's command are not impossibly at odds. I do have an innate and powerful tendency toward anger. I am tempted more strongly than others in the direction of hostile confrontation and even physical aggression. I, more often than others, feel the great desire to kick somebody's butt. God has given me a heavy challenge. And He has allowed the enemy a significant opportunity to tempt me. But it is not unfair for God to expect me to withstand that temptation and, though I may be fiercely angry, not to sin by taking a shovel to some fool's head – or otherwise violently acting out my bipolar anger.

God, through Christ's death and resurrection, has given me the grace to turn from that and all temptation. (I sin when I ignore the grace that God provides to overcome the temptation.) He has given me a bipolar brain, but He has also given me His Holy Spirit – the same Holy Spirit who raised Christ from the dead. And the Holy Spirit who lives in me is far greater than any bipolar temptation. And the temptation is an opportunity for me to demonstrate my love for God through my obedience to His command – in spite of my genetic pre-disposition to disobey the command. Indeed, the genetic pre-disposition to literally smack somebody makes my obedience to the command not to smack an even greater demonstration of my love for God. I would imagine that the greater the temptation, the greater the smile on God's face when we conquer the temptation - by relying on His all-sufficient grace.

With this recognition, I return to my original question of how a Christian is called to relate to a homosexual.

The simple answer: Love.

And I hear the question, "But what about the sin? Don't we have to call sin for what it is? Sin. And it *is* a sin to act out homosexual temptation, right?"

Yes. All true.

"So, how do we call sin "sin" and still love the sinner?"

First, I would acknowledge that it is just as much of a sin for me to have sex with a woman not my wife as it is for two men to have sex with each other. And, since I am single... I, just as the homosexual, must find a way to go without.

Second, I want to acknowledge that it does seem to be a real hardship to be gay in a world that is largely heterosexual. It is one thing to have your behavior called sin. It is quite another to be ostracized by family and friends to the point of being unable to openly state who you are.

I am certain that gays are treated much more fairly today than in the past. If they were not there would not even be a discussion about gay marriage and a protest in front of a church might well be met with a sinful violence. But even though things are better, hatred does still exist. I have heard the nasty comments and the cruel jokes told behind the backs of homosexuals and I have seen a man marched out of a locker room because he was gay. I don't know whether he had done anything taboo.

I am a Christian and do call homosexual behavior a sin, but it also seems to me to be a painful life. And I've had enough pain of my own to be able to see it in others and want not to unduly add to it.

Third, I would want my homosexual friend to know the gospel message. I want him to have a lived experience of the gospel message. I want him to know that although the Bible does call homosexual acts a sin, God sent His Son, Jesus Christ, to set us free from our sins by dying on the Cross the death that we deserve. I want to tell him that I fully believe that God loves him just as much as He loves me and that when he gives his life to Christ he will have eternal life in paradise. That the Holy Spirit will come to dwell in him and the joy and peace and love of Christ will always be available to him. And I want my still gay friend to know that once he has embraced Christ, the Holy Spirit will empower him to be the man God calls him to be.

I want my gay friend to know that he can turn to Christ even while he is still a sinner because I know that "while we were still sinners, Christ died for us." (Romans 5:8)

See, I don't think I need to deal all that much with the sin. I would affirm that, yes, God really does call homosexual behavior a sin. I would not back away one inch from that truth. But if my friend knows that I am a Christian, he probably already has a pretty good sense that I consider gay sex a sin.

What I need to do is love my gay friend as I assertively, but gently, address the sin. I need to be the love of Christ to him. I need to sincerely and joyfully live the gospel message in front of him. I need to show him – by my behavior - the peace and freedom and strength that I have in Christ. I need to so manifest the love and joy and truth of Christ that my friend will not be able to turn away from Him. I need to lead my friend to the point of embracing Christ and, then, support him as he grows in his faith. And, then, the Holy Spirit living in my friend will deal with the sin – as He has done with all who give their lives to Christ.

Many times, I did not want to believe that my angry bipolar behavior was a sin. I believed it was justified. I was wrong. But it was not being condemned for my angry outbursts and arguments that turned my life around. Yes, I needed to be told that my ranting, out-of-control actions were sin, but it was love that turned me to Christ. And it was Christ who changed my life – and behavior.

If not for bipolar, I would not have this specific understanding of the innate temptations some others face. It is a blessing.

CHAPTER 25

BONE-BREAKING BLESSINGS, PART II

I am not finding much blessing today in my busted ankle or bipolar disorder.

It has been sixteen days since I broke my right ankle. It will be another eleven before I see the orthopedist, hoping to hear him say the sacred words. "Pick up your mat and throw those cursed crutches to the ground." It will not be a moment too soon. I sent them flying a couple of times today. And, no, I am not such a 'holy man writing a Christian book' that I did it without cussing them as they soared. I do have quite a vocabulary to tame. And a bipolar anger that gives full-throat to the coarser dialects.

Yes, the cursing, the pitching of the crutches, the wrongly expressed anger – they were all sins. I am still the wretched man of Romans chapter 7.

The frustration of stumbling around on one leg built up over the last three days. It was not something that I was dwelling upon. It built slowly, insidiously, on the fringe of my awareness. I was not losing my temper, but I was noticing myself having more frequently to quickly check my emotions when I dropped a crutch, spilled a drink I was too clumsy to carry, or stumbled over the boot-cast which I have come to know as Darth Vader.

I tried to focus on the Lord. I remembered the joyful 10 year-old boy with the cut Achilles tendon. I tried to remember that God is, indeed, blessing me in all of this. I remembered that my neighbor has it far worse than me. He has compound fractures (that's bone through the skin, folks) of three bones in his foot and ankle. Poor me. I'll be running and climbing on this ankle for months before my neighbor can get out of a cast. I prayed. I went to church and worshipped. I told myself that God has blessings in this for me.

And still the crutches flew and the cussing roared. And I broke the boredom of being hobbled by taking "comfort' in the old reliable lie – lust.

I am not at my best.

"So, Mr. Blessed with Bipolar," I challenge myself in anger, "where is the blessing in all of this? I can't see it and I sure don't feel it. *Blessing*?! Yeah. It's a bunch of crap." And that raises another question. "Do I <u>need</u> to see and feel and understand a blessing in order to be blessed? Can it just be - without me ever noticing it?"

The same blessings are here today in the broken-ankle-boredom and bipolar disorder that were here yesterday and last week. It is still a chance to learn and know that I can have Christ's peace and joy even when I am unable to run, climb, use an elliptical machine, walk unhindered, or drive. Even if I gain ten pounds. It is still a chance to give my body a rest. A chance to deal with this frustration in a way that gives glory to God and lets shine the light of Christ.

Today, I chose to turn away from the blessings of bipolar disorder and busted bones. And, today, I do not see the blessings. I don't feel them. But the blessings are here, nonetheless, and I don't quite understand. God is here and loves me just as much as He was there and loved me in yesterday's church service – regardless of whether I feel His Presence or how I behave or what attitudes I choose to keep on choosing.

I say, "God tear down this wall that I have built. Tear down my sin. 'Wash me, and I will be whiter than snow . . . Create in me a clean heart, O God, and renew a steadfast spirit within me. Do not cast me from your presence or take your Holy Spirit from me. Restore to me the joy of your salvation and grant me a willing spirit, to sustain me.' " (Psalm 51: 7b,10-12)

And God says, "Praise."

And I am blessed.

CHAPTER 26

A TIME FOR MADNESS

There are times that require a man who is willing to do something nuts. By the grace of God, I am well-equipped for such occasions.

I had just walked off the beach at Hollywood, Florida when I realized that if I wanted to make it to the Miami airport in time to catch my flight home to Pittsburgh, I was going to need to do something a little off the rails.

It was October of 2004 and the beach was hot and gorgeous. But I was not on vacation. One day earlier I had participated in a settlement conference with three attorneys (none of whom were representing me) as part of my breach of contract case against St. Thomas University. The conference yielded nothing in the way of progress toward a settlement, but the attorneys did get to see that I was not the raving lunatic that their client had portrayed me to be. Getting to the airport, however, was going to require me to make a withdrawal on my ample reserve of madness. I was desperate and the situation demanded a quick decision and bold action.

I had scheduled an extra day in Florida to unwind and enjoy the sunshine after the settlement conference. It was a good idea. Given the fact that I had no prospects for full-time employment, I wasn't going to be making another Florida trip any time soon. And, since it was the end of October and I was headed back to Pittsburgh, I was not likely to see the sun again until sometime in March – for an hour or two. So, I got up early – that was 9:00AM for me – and did a twenty-minute water-treading workout in the pool of the Days Inn at Pompano, then packed my bags, hopped in the Chevy minivan I had as a rental upgrade, and headed for the beach at Hollywood. I had always loved it there. It was my refuge when I lived on-campus at St. Thomas University – a safe haven from the not-so-hidden evils of law school.

I parked the van on a narrow side street and, knowing that I had to be at the airport in just a couple of hours, I quickly fed the meter and headed for the beach.

I smelled the salty breeze and I was awash in the same peace the Hollywood beach had given me four years earlier when I would escape the law school three times a week. I walked a couple of miles, stopped in a few of the chaotic shops along the paved broadwalk where every language known to man is spoken, and had lunch in an open-air seafood restaurant, the name of which I forgot the moment I left.

I had met a waitress in that restaurant the night before. She was about my age, maybe 40, and the only reason I returned for lunch. While I was waiting for my dinner the previous night, she wandered over and caught me reading my Bible. I don't remember much of what we said to each other, but I do recall that her eyes were dark, her hair was long, and I liked her. She told me that she had just moved to South Florida, but did not explain. I sensed that there was something she had needed to leave behind. I told her that I was there to go to the mediation conference. I copped to the scandal of being expelled and, since she didn't run away, I kept talking. There was something about the lines on her face that said, "strength," and I found that beautiful. I imagined that she had seen her own share of troubles, but her dark eyes smiled, nonetheless. And I liked her.

The waitress noticed my Bible and said so. And, naturally, that got me to talking even more. I am not sure what I said, but it had to be something about how I can't make it through a day without Christ and need to be "in the Word." It turned out that she, too, was a Spirit-filled, whacky tongue-speakin', not-of-this-world, Assembly-of-God-type. Just like me.

I couldn't shake the feeling that the waitress seemed a little lost, sort of sadly dreaming of some other kind of life. I must have said something that indicated what I felt I was picking up from her. (It happens sometimes whether I want it to or not.) And she told me that she didn't feel quite right without her Bible. She had looked through everything for it when she unpacked from moving, but couldn't find it. I said quite obviously, "Well, it looks like it's time to get a new one." She looked back just as obviously with a "no-kiddin'" smirk and said something about hoping to find the old one or not having had the time to look for a book store since moving. So, as I left that little ramshackle, ocean-side fish-stand, I knew I had a mission. As I said, the waitress was the only reason I returned for lunch the next day.

But this is a chapter about having to do something crazy and there was nothing crazy about the hot waitress and me. No one-night stand. No mad sex with a nameless mystery, never to be seen again. I just bought a Bible for a sister in Christ who seemed a little unsettled. I knew that I would never see her again, but I was pleased that God had put us in each other's path just to say to me, "Don't worry. I have people in this town, too – where you've come to pick a fight."

Just by noticing my Bible and speaking up, the waitress encouraged me. God used us to be the love of Christ to each other for a split-second in time. Such a small thing made a difference. Maybe she remembers when she picks up the Bible I gave her.

The waitress made me know that God was going with me into that mediation conference and just to make me absolutely sure, God put a man in place to witness to me in a Publix grocery store later that night. After all of that, how could I allow my sister to go without the Word of God?

However, when I left the restaurant after lunch the next afternoon, the madness was yet to be required of me.

I needed to get to the airport and I had left myself just enough time to return the rented van and catch the shuttle bus. I made my way back up the beach, reluctantly heading for everything that follows November Pittsburgh. I was in no great rush to leave Florida at that time of year, but I had not realized how wildly eager I must have been to get to the ocean. I had been in such a hurry to get out of the van and onto the beach that not only had I locked the keys in the van, I had also left the engine running and the radio blasting. (No! I am not absent-minded. Just the opposite. Sometimes there is so much scrambling around up there that trivialities like stopping the engine and taking the keys before locking the doors get lost in the mental traffic.)

Suddenly, I was in real danger of missing the flight home and not having a place to stay. I walked down the busy main road and around construction, searching for a pay phone. (I had not yet found any need for a cell and still don't use it for much except the clock.) I called the police and explained the situation. They recommended that I call a "wrecker." (Fortunately, I had spent enough time with my sisters in Tennessee to know that "wrecker" is southern for "tow-truck.")

So, I called an auto repair shop and waited. And waited. And paced around the construction. And cursed – which, somehow, did not make the "wrecker" show up. And waited. More and more anxiously pacing, fruitlessly cursing, and building up a potential tirade-panic. When, suddenly! – a gem of bipolar inspiration struck in timely fashion. I cranked up and pitched a chunk of concrete rubble through the passenger window and I was off to the airport quicker than anyone could needlessly dial 9-1-1.

It may not have been the most Christ-like option, but neither would have been missing the flight and charging a later one to my old man's credit card.

I sped unlimited down I-95 just like everybody else in South Florida (I was, however, one of the vehicles on the correct side of the road) and jumped out of the van as soon as I hit the rental place. I ran to the shuttle bus without stopping to explain the absence of the passenger window or the concrete and glass all over the seat. I made it to the airport just in time and soothed my conscience with the thought that I had saved the cost of an additional airfare and maybe another night in a hotel and one day's car rental fee.

My conscience, however, was not so easily soothed and when I got home I called the rental company. I explained why I had put the chunk of concrete through the passenger window and asked them to send me a bill. They never did. God looks out for the mentally handicapped!

A less bipolar man would have missed that flight.

CHAPTER 27

BIPOLAR BOLDNESS

My mouth cannot always keep the bipolar from jumping off my tongue. My extreme emotions have led me into a number of heated conversations. Some of those "debates" have cost me jobs, a law school scholarship, and maybe some friends. But those passionate, heart-felt, sometimes bitter disagreements have gone a long way toward training me in the differences between being aggressive, being passive, and being effectively assertive. I am getting better at it, however, I am still quite capable of blowing my lid.

On the other hand, my mother has said that she sometimes misses my manic "excitability" that has been so well-treated with lamictal. It's still there. I am just getting better at only using it as a strategic deployment.

The interpersonal conflicts I have had in and through bipolar agitation have forced me to work at dealing more effectively with strong disagreements about passionately held convictions. I have no desire to lose any more jobs or get thrown out of any more schools. However, the past 46 years have taught me that although I will agree with some of the people all of the time and all of the people some of the time, there will most times be some crackpot who simply refuses bipolar wisdom. Now, I do pray, "Lord, make me quick to listen, slow to speak, and slow to get angry," but it is entirely unreasonable for me to expect myself to always keep my mouth shut.

Therefore, in the service of getting along in this world without surrendering _or_ exploding, I have had to work on being assertive. Like I said, I am getting better, but . . .

Aggressiveness means personally attacking, insulting, or intentionally intimidating the other individual in an attempt to "win" the argument by forcing them to capitulate. It can work if all you want to do is stand up, be heard, and make your point with such ferocity that it will never be forgotten. The downside to this approach is that it is unlikely to persuade anybody and it could cost you some friends and respect. Also, if you get a reputation for that kind of verbal aggression, people may become unwilling to tell you when they disagree. That might sound nice and peaceful, but it would preclude any honest relationship. And if others feel like they cannot say to your face what they are thinking, they are likely – human nature being 'human' – to tell it to somebody else behind your back. Perhaps your boss – or college dean. And they are unlikely to limit their disclosure to the truth and nothing but the truth.

Letting your aggression loose right in the teeth of some fool who may well have it coming does feel good in the moment. But the long-term consequences can be more trouble than it's worth – and long indeed. Finding a new job can take months. And every time I have blown up on somebody – even when I was completely in the right and justified – I have ended up feeling some guilt. And after an angry blow-up, guilt can lead the bipolar into depression. I do not need that.

It took much trial and error for me to learn the above and even more to be convinced. I do want to avoid those ranting, loud, insulting fights, but simply walking away is often not best when the issue truly matters and the person is important.

Passivity means being unwilling – or unable – to stand up for what you believe in or what you want in a given situation. You give up your own legitimate, earnest convictions in order to avoid any sort of conflict and make sure that everybody is pleased with you. It keeps everybody thinking you're a 'niceguy.' And it tears out a little piece of your heart.

I have at times been passive. Those occasions that come quickly to mind are the times when I have failed to take advantage of an opportunity to tell somebody about Christ and my relationship with Him. That, for me, usually has much to do with not wanting to make the other person uncomfortable or have them think that I have lost my mind. (Little do they know). Whenever I have gone passive like that, it has left me feeling small and weak. "God, forgive me for the times when I have been ashamed of you. Make me to speak up boldly for You and Your Word."

Passivity can be effective if the beliefs or desires in that given situation are not important enough to you to risk a conflict that could harm a relationship. But if you are giving up on something that matters or repeatedly going along with the crowd without sufficiently expressing your own point of view or preference, sooner or later, you are going to pay a price.

You may get walked on.

You may get so fed up that you finally lash out and become overly aggressive, costing yourself a job or a relationship. (I have tried to bury anger in the hope of avoiding conflict only to have it blow like an exploding pressure cooker fierce with boiling fat. There are consequences.)

You may become passive-aggressive, semiconsciously taking calm and quiet shots at people to get revenge – a time-tested way to subtly sabotage a relationship.

Assertiveness means firmly making your point or requesting what you need without attacking the other person. You stay focused on the issue rather than the person. You listen to what the other has to say. And you are willing to admit that they may have some good points. You're open to compromise, but not to the point of being walked over or sacrificing what is essential to you.

Repeatedly yelling, pointing, and/or cursing is likely a sign that you are crossing out of assertion and into aggression. That heat rising in your head and thumping in your chest probably means that it's time to check the gauges. If you feel the veins bulging in your temple and throat and you have any desire to save the relationship, go immediately to operation shutdown (See, Chapter 16) – and apologize, not necessarily for the argument, but at least for not handling it with less hostility. I've been there. Many times. It happens. Apologize, repent, and be forgiven.

For the person who has bipolar disorder, assertiveness would appear to be an especially difficult skill to master. Our seismic emotions and sudden mood swings are not given to stepping back, taking a deep breath, and formulating an effective strategy for delivering a passionate, persuasive, and _respectful_ argument. We are more likely to hold our convictions so strongly that we feel compelled to burst forth with all the bipolar energy we can muster. [I cherish that passion. But I must harness (not bury or deny) it for that passion to do any good.] For those same reasons, we who have bipolar disorder have even greater reason, and opportunity, to master the skill of assertiveness.

My bipolar emotions still get me into heated "debates." Swearing that off would drown out my soul. I have been, and still am, aggressive, assertive, and (when I am too depressed to care) passive. But I'm working on it.

Below is a semi-fictional, non-verbatim composite of several conversations in which I think I held the balance, remained assertive, and respectfully but passionately made my point. As always, you be the judge.

My friend, Ephraim, like me, is no stranger to vigorous debate. And I have challenged him on the great and unavoidable question: "Who do you think Jesus Christ is?" Some may give it only passing consideration, but, somewhere along the line, everybody gives a definitive and life-changing answer.

Ephraim is a young man, but he is likely closer to the grave than me. It was time for Ephraim to be pressed on the most important question he will ever face. Knowing that Jesus is the only way to heaven, I would not have been much of a friend if I didn't do the pressing. Far better to offend than let a friend go head-long into hell.

Ephraim has known for years that I am a Christian and he makes it easy for me to discuss salvation. He brings it up.

"You know," ponders Ephraim aloud, "I have great respect for Jesus."

Now, Ephraim knows full-well that statement is not going to drift past me and out on into the ether. And I know that he knows those words are going to raise my brow. I assume that he is looking for a discussion.

"Yes," I popped up, grinning. "I do, too."

He laughed. "No kiddin'."

"Why do you respect him?" I pressed.

"He was a great teacher and a man of peace," Ephraim said.

I asked him what teachings of Jesus that he liked.

"Love your neighbor as yourself" he frowned. "There aren't many people who follow that."

"Yeah, we all fall pretty short."

"See, if people who followed Jesus really lived like that . . ."

"Christians are sinners, Ephraim. Even me. That's why Jesus came. God knew we couldn't save ourselves so He sent Jesus to do it for us."

"I'm a man of peace," said Ephraim. "I don't see how Christians could be for going to war. Jesus said, 'Love your neighbor. Didn't He say to love your enemies?' He was a man of peace."

"He did say, 'Love your enemies,' but He was more than a man of peace. He died on the cross to pay the penalty for our sins."

Ephraim nodded. "He would be against going to war."

"There are a number of times in the Old Testament where God commands Israel to go to war and wipe out their enemies," I offered.

Ephraim did not like that. "I don't believe a lot of those Old Testament stories."

Ephraim and I had been down similar roads before. This time I wanted to challenge him. Call it a moment of bipolar boldness.

"Eph, you say you respect Jesus and you use some of his teachings to bolster your arguments and, then, in the next breath you call him a liar."

Ephraim's bone-thin frame looked like it stretched up six inches. His eyes crossed. He sighed, laughed, and raised his voice all in one incredulous breath. "What? How did I do that? I didn't call Jesus a liar."

"You say you don't believe in the Old Testament."

"That's right. Not all of it," Ephraim shot back. "Jesus is not the Old Testament."

"Jesus said that He is the fulfillment of the Old Testament law and prophets. You know, Genesis, Moses, the Psalms."

[The discussion is now becoming difficult. We are confronting our disagreement head-on. Neither of us is pointing or cursing, but we are speaking firmly and more loudly than when we started. We are not yet overly aggressive and my bipolar self is not about to let me go passive. This matter is too important.]

Ephraim shook his head with a short jerk and tightened his lips. "Okay. What does that mean? Jesus is not in the Old Testament."

"You say you respect Jesus, but don't believe the Old Testament. How is that consistent with Jesus saying that He came not to abolish the law and the prophets, but to fulfill them?"

Ephraim stopped. He squinted and laughed nervously, searching for words.

Ephraim is a kind and caring, peace-loving man. (On that score, he is a good example to Christians) He has seen my anger and remained a friend when bipolar was booming thunder in my brain. But he is not a push-over and there are places where we deeply disagree. If we couldn't do that out-loud and assertively with each other and remain friends, then we really never were friends at all.

Bipolar gave me a push and I repeated. "It's *not* consistent to say that you respect Jesus, but don't believe the Old Testament." I clenched my jaw and stared, waiting for Ephraim to respond.

"I don't know the Bible like you do," he argued.

"So read it. You'll see that Jesus can't just be a great prophet or teacher."

"Why not?"

We had challenged each other. But what Ephraim did not know is that I have forced myself to look at Jesus through the eyes of an unbeliever. The question, "What if Jesus is not the Son of God, but just a prophet and teacher," was not new to me. I was ready to respond or, rather, God had prepared me and the Holy Spirit was about to give me words.

"Jesus cannot just be a great prophet or teacher," I said, "because his greatest prophecy and teaching was that He was the one and only Son of God. That He would die to pay the penalty for the sins of all mankind. That He is the Savior of the world who would rise from the dead.

"If you say that He was not the Son of God, the Savior, that He did not rise from the dead, then you are saying that He was wrong about His most important prophecies and teachings. If you're right, then Jesus is either a liar or a lunatic, but He is certainly not – if you are right that He is not the Son of God – then He is certainly not a great prophet." (Lewis, 1952, p.52)

"That's your faith," he protested. "You have faith."

"Yes. I do. Absolutely," I said, staring with an up-to-something grin, "But I also have logic."

"What logic? Ephraim yelped, grinned, and teased. "You believe and I don't."

"Logic. Yes, I believe. And here's my logic," I pressed with a now wild grin. "Jesus prophesied that He was the Son of God who would die for the forgiveness of sin and then rise from the dead. Therefore, if Jesus was not the Son of God, He was dead wrong about His most important prophecies. Great prophets are not wrong about their most important prophecies. *Therefore*, if Jesus was wrong about His most important prophecy, then He was not a great prophet . . . That's the cold, hard logic behind my belief," I declared.

Ephraim sighed. "That . . . Rich, does not prove that Jesus is the Son of God."

"No, it doesn't. It proves – logically - that He could not just be a great prophet."

"So, you believe that Jesus is the Son of God. You *believe*. Just like I said before," Ephraim reiterated. "You *believe*."

"*Logic*! Ephraim," I exclaimed, "*Logic* demands that Jesus is either a liar, a lunatic, or the Lord God of all creation." (Lewis, 1952, p.52)

Ephraim was in a bit of a quandary. He truly does respect Jesus as a man. He believes that Jesus lived a life of peace, that He loved others, and that if we all followed the teachings of Christ, this world would be heaven on earth. Ephraim did not like the liar or lunatic choice and, like most people educated in the twentieth century, he places big value on logic.

"Well, you see," Ephraim said more slowly and without the same fire, "I don't know. I hope, but that's not the same as believing. I don't believe."

"You're in trouble," I challenged with whatever small compassion I could muster in the middle of a rough debate. As a friend, I needed to let Ephraim know the very long-term consequences of his choice not to believe.

We stared at each other.

"You're in trouble, Ephraim," I repeated. "And I'm worried about you."

"You don't have to worry about me," he whispered firmly.

"Hell is a long time." I looked straight-faced right in his eyes.

Ephraim stopped dead. His head drew back and he stared at me, wide-eyed.

Ephraim and I had known each other quite awhile and we had been down this road before. It was time to smack him right between the equivocations with the genuine consequences of what he did or did not believe.

"You think I'm going to hell," he winced incredulously, jerking his head. He smiled oddly and I imagined that he wanted me to back off.

"I know that you told me that you don't believe. And I know that the only way to heaven is to put your faith in Jesus Christ as the Savior of the world and surrender your life to Him."

"Would Jesus go to war?" Ephraim cracked, fighting back against his eternal dilemma.

Maybe I should not have let him suck me in. But I had made my point and I knew that he was not about to forget it. I wanted to answer his questions. Maybe I went passive. It was not a completely comfortable discussion for me and I probably wanted, as much as Ephraim, to seek more tranquil ground. So we talked about war.

Ephraim persisted, "Well, would Jesus go to war?"

"Jesus drove the money-changers out of the temple, overturned their tables, scattered their coins, and took a whip to their sheep and cattle." (John 2:14-15) Sounds to me like He was fully capable of blowing His righteous stack."

"So, Jesus had a mean streak?' He asked sarcastically and firmly grinned without a trace of bitterness.

I did not say anything.

"So, did Jesus have a mean streak?" He was not about to let me off easy after the way I had challenged him. I respect that. Ephraim is a good debater, but his heart was not made for law school.

"I'm telling you what Jesus did," I said. "He made a whip out of cords and used it to drive merchants out of the temple."

I wanted to make the point that Jesus was no light-weight pansy.

Ephraim was not satisfied. And he had every right not to be. "Are you saying that Jesus would go to war?"

"I'm telling you that in the Old Testament there are times when God commanded Israel to go in and take the land of other peoples and wipe them out."

"I don't believe a lot of those stories," said Ephraim.

"Then don't use Jesus to support your arguments," I smiled and smirked, "Because He not only believed those stories, He said that He is the fulfillment of them."

Ephraim went back again to the easier ground of war. "Don't you see?" he said, "War is the most horrific thing man does. Why does this country have to have the hammer to pound on everybody?" (It's a legitimate question. And I believe that our government must be forced to justify the use of that hammer every time we pound it, but I thank God we have it.)

"When is there a time for war?" I asked. "When is it right to go to war?"

"Right?" he questioned, apparently stunned by my implication that war could ever be just.

"Yes. When is it right to go to war?"

Ephraim appeared to be more at ease now that the discussion had shifted from his eternal plight. He pounced on his chance to criticize George W. Bush and the hierarchy of the American military.

"Don't you understand that we are just using our military to exert our will on other countries?"

"Seems to me there are times when that is good and times when it's bad," I responded. "But you're not answering my question. When is it right to go to war?"

Ephraim refused to say whether he thought that war could ever be justified. Not wanting to answer the question either way, he said, "We need to talk with our enemies. We've done things to make them angry?"

"And what do we do when talking doesn't work?" I tilted, brow raised.

Ephraim shook his head and smirked.

I tried to re-focus the conversation. "We're losing track of the Jesus question," I said.

"Yes. You believe that He is the Son of God and the Savior of the world, but you say He would approve of going to war."

"And you say He's a great teacher and too nice a guy to ever go to war," I responded.

"That's right. God is love. How could Jesus be the Son of a loving God and go to war?"

"How could He not?"

"How could He not?!" Ephraim nearly shrieked, "War is not love!"

"I do understand your position, Ephraim," I said, trying to get back to being calm and maintain some 'reflective-listening-seminar-type' rapport. "War is horrific and you're a deeply caring man. You want to be a man of peace, a pacifist."

"I am a pacifist," Ephraim proudly reiterated. "That's one reason why I won't be going back for a law degree."

"Yes, you are. And you're right – God is love. But He is also justice and righteousness. And, yes, truth – and wisdom, too." I steered clear of the 'God Is On Our Side' discussion.

I continued, "But there is evil in the world. The truth is, there is evil in every one of us. We are born sinners."

"I don't know that we're born sinners," Ephraim mildly protested, "But, of course, we all do bad things. Break the commandments."

"Let me get biblical on ya for a second, Eph."

He took a deep breath and stared. I took that as permission.

"God is sinless, perfect, holy."

"Right. I believe that. I believe in God," Ephraim insisted.

"I know. You believe in some kind of God. But I'm talking about the God of the Bible. The God who has revealed Himself to us in the Bible. You agree with me that He is sinless, perfect, and holy."

Ephraim nodded quickly.

"And I am telling you that He is so holy that He is completely separated from sin. He can't even look upon it."

"Okay. Makes sense. I guess."

"And since He is – and must be – completely separated from sin, then our sin separates us from Him. When we sin, we separate ourselves from God – who is holy."

"Yeah," Ephraim cocked his head with a question mark.

"And since we're all sinners – like you said – that puts us all in a pretty desperate situation. Separated from God. In fact, I would say that 'eternal separation from God' is the precise circumstance of the people in hell."

"Yeah, where you think I'm headed."

"It's not what God wants for anybody," I quickly reassured. "He is love and He is always willing to forgive. But because He is also righteousness and justice, He must also punish sin. If He didn't, He would deny His own holiness. Not punishing sin would make God a liar. He can't say, 'Alright, you're sin isn't so bad. I'll let you come on in and spend eternity with me.' He can't do that because it would make Him unholy."

"I don't know about all this," Ephraim pondered slowly, shaking his head.

"But God *is* love. And He *does* want to spend eternity with us in paradise. He wants us to praise Him and share His glory. It's why He made us."

"So, we say we're sorry. He forgives us and we all go to heaven," Ephraim argued with a chuckling grin.

"Just skip the consequences and head on into heaven?" I challenged.

"Sounds good to me."

"But God says there are consequences. In fact, He says, 'The wages of sin is death.'"

"We all die," Ephraim countered. "If death is the penalty for sin, then we all pay it."

"He's talking about eternal death. Not just a dead body, a dead spirit separated from God and every good thing - forever."

"So, we're back to me in hell," Ephraim stared, tight-lipped.

"That is the penalty for sin. But, like you said, God is love. He loves us so much that He sent His

Son to pay the penalty we deserve so we can be forgiven and go to heaven."

"Yeah, if – *if* we believe that's true, then we go to heaven." Ephraim shook his head.

"No. If I believe it *and* embrace what Christ did for me on the Cross and ask Him to be my Savior and ask Him to take control of my life and be my Lord, then my sins are forgiven. "

"And that's the only way to heaven?"

"Do you know anybody else who lived a perfect, sinless life and then died to pay the penalty for your sin? *And* rose from the dead?!"

Ephraim bit his lip.

"That's why I said that you're in trouble. Because the only other option is to pay the penalty yourself."

Ephraim paused. This was not all new to him. Maybe I used different words, but he had heard the gist of salvation before and found a way to reason that it isn't *all* true. He took some time to remind himself, then returned to more comfortable ground.

"All of that still doesn't explain war and how you think God could approve of it."

I foolishly took the bait again. Maybe Ephraim really should go back for that law degree.

"God gave us free will. And people use that gift to choose to do evil. And, sometimes, that evil is so great that, to save lives, it has to be stopped. And, sometimes, the only way for man to stop evil is to choose to go to war against it. Wasn't it an act of love to stop the holocaust?"

"We need to talk with our enemies," Ephraim insisted, "We have done things to make them hate us."

And with that, I was sucked in again. I am not the quintessential bipolar-ly bold debater. I am not always perfectly assertive. I am learning. Years ago Ephraim and I might have been on the edge of a fist-fight. Yes, a fist-fight over Christ. I <u>do</u> have bipolar. Crazy things do happen. Not as often these days, but they do happen.

This time, I went passive and allowed myself to be moved off of the increasingly uneasy salvation discussion.

"When is there a time to go to war," I said, trying to frame Ephraim. "Is it ever right to go to war?"

Ephraim knew where I was headed and he plowed a fork in the road.

"This war in Iraq should never have been started."

Not exactly an answer to my question, but I could not help biting.

"Sadaam Hussein invaded Kuwait in 1990. U.N. and U.S. forces went in and forced him out of Kuwait. In 1991, Sadaam signed a peace treaty in which he agreed to allow weapons inspectors into Iraq."

"Yeah, weapons of mass destruction. Our excuse to start a war."

"We know that he had weapons of mass destruction."

"What?!" Ephraim snapped, astounded that I could make such a statement. "Where did you get that?"

"He used chemical weapons on his own people. Those are weapons of mass destruction. Then he breached the peace treaty by not allowing weapons inspectors into the country. Over 12 years, he violated 17 or 18 U.N. resolutions. Finally, the President told him that the U.S. would use the military to enforce the treaty and the resolutions. We gave him how many months to comply with that ultimatum? He ignored it. So, Bush backed up his talk, did the 'shock and awe,' and took Sadaam out of power. But that's not the issue you and I are getting at."

"Bush just wanted to go to war and he was going to find a way to do it no matter what happened," Ephraim protested, in agreement with many Americans, who, thank God, have that right.

"My question is still, 'When is it right to go to war?'"

"We shouldn't be in Iraq."

I was not getting a straight answer, so I took an indirect route.

"Okay," I said, "Did Hitler have to be stopped?"

"I don't know. He shouldn't have been allowed to get so far. He should have been stopped sooner."

"So, it would have been right to go to war against Hitler sooner than we did?"

"We should use diplomacy."

"You think the U.S. should sit down and talk with the leader of *Iran* (?!) who has publicly said that he wants to wipe Israel off the map?"

"Well, no, we can't talk with him."

"So, what do we do, let him blow-up Israel?"

"Why is it always about Israel?"

"Because this guy said he wants to wipe Israel off the map. If he said it about one of our other allies, I'd talk about them."

"Why should we have the hammer to pound down another nation?"

"Because they said they want to wipe our ally off the map and they are trying to build a nuke to be able to do it."

"Israel is a rogue nation."

"Israel doesn't hijack civilian planes and slam them into civilian skyscrapers. Should we not fight terrorism, either?!"

Bipolar boldness had taken me far off the topic of salvation, but without it the entire conversation may have never happened and neither Ephraim nor I would have been forced to examine and defend our positions. Bipolar boldness led me to take on a debate of powerful issues and struggle to articulate my beliefs. That's a good thing.

"Do you think that it could ever be right to go to war?"

"*Right*?!" Ephraim cracked with a rising pitch that zipped, "How could war *ever* be *right*?"

"Should Hitler have been stopped?" I popped.

"Why is it always Hitler?"

"Because you say there is never a reason to go to war and Hitler is the most extreme example. Were we right to stop Hitler?"

He said nothing.

"Ephraim, should we have stopped Hitler?" I demanded.

"War is horrific, Rich. There is always another way."

I shook my head and blinked. "You can't say that it was right to go to war against Hitler?!" I squinted, still shaking my head.

There was not much left to say without screaming and name-calling. By the grace of God I somehow realized that neither was going to change Ephraim's mind or bring him to Christ. That's a profound recognition for a man with bipolar disorder in the midst of an assertive debate of bedrock issues and core beliefs. This stuff mattered to me and, when Ephraim could not say that it was right to go to war against Hitler, my natural, bipolar inclination really was to scream and name-call. But I walked away. There was nothing left to say. Ephraim and I were simply not going to agree and beating each other over the head was not going to change that – or, most importantly, bring Ephraim to Christ.

It was a heated, uncomfortable, and even combative debate, but it was assertive rather than aggressive. We strongly stated our beliefs, made our arguments, and listened to each other with a fair amount of respect rather than attacking each other. We stayed focused on the issues without insulting each other. (Sure, we both thought the other made some idiotic comments, but neither of us called the other an idiot.)

Because Ephraim and I did not take the easy route and passively avoid this difficult discussion, we now know how strongly we disagree. Because we were assertive and not aggressive, Ephraim and I are still friends.

Through this conversation I learned some things about my own beliefs. I was forced to think on my feet and put into cogent words the reasons for what I believe. Because of this debate I am better prepared for the next similar one and, perhaps, I know myself and Ephraim a little better. Maybe I gave him something to think about, too. Maybe. For the sake of his eternal soul, I pray the Holy Spirit gives Ephraim a whole lot more to think about.

And I am not sure that I would have had the nerve or desire for any of this conversation if I did not have bipolar disorder and the screwball boldness that sometimes comes along with it.

Minding my own business is not one of the blessings of bipolar disorder. Sometimes I simply cannot keep myself from intruding on a conversation that piques my mania. So, I here present another non-verbatim, semi-fictional composite of a bipolar-ly bold conversation that actually did happen.

I was sitting comfortably in the food court of Ross Park Mall and writing when I heard blaring behind me the self-assured voice of a thin and bearded, gray-haired professor: "I cannot comprehend," he crowingly declared, "how any educated person could believe in creationism!"

Slowly, I turned.

"Excuse me," I intruded to the 'outspoken' gentleman seated with three others. "I don't mean to intrude," I said, spinning the truth on its head, "but I overheard your conversation and I wanted to say that I have a masters degree in existential psychology and I spent a year in law school and I <u>do</u> believe in creationism."

"So what?" cracked the gray-bearded gentleman in a way that I imagined said anger. "The fact that you believe it in spite of your education doesn't make it true."

"No, it doesn't," I agreed, grinning. "I just wanted you to know that I am a living example of the kind of person that you just can't imagine exists."

"Well, It's no surprise to me that people like you do exist. I just can't comprehend how somebody with your education can believe what you claim to believe."

Suddenly, I went from unwitting hypo-pleasant-manic mode into bipolar genius mode. (I am **NOT** saying that I am a genius. But I have learned how to pretend. Or, as a professor of mine once said, "I have learned how to sound like the Pope on issues about which I know very little." My father, on the other hand, would say that it has something to do with bovine digestion.)

"Well," I drew back with a leering glance and just a little more bass in my voice, "The fact that you have a limited ability to comprehend what I believe does not make it *un*true."

That sounded worse than I had intended and it stung.

"There's no need to be insulting," the gentleman replied.

He was right and I shakily tried to soften and clarify my remark. "I don't mean to be insulting. You said that you cannot comprehend what I believe. And I want you to know that I only brought up my education because you said that you couldn't understand how educated people can believe in creation. I think I sounded arrogant. I don't want that."

"No. I understood that. But let me ask you, how can you not believe in evolution?"

"*Believe* in evolution?" I asked.

"You believe in creationism."

"Yes. I'm a Christian."

"So, you don't believe in evolution."

I hesitated, searching for words.

"I am not claiming to know precisely how God created the heavens and the earth."

"The Bible says He did it all in six days, right?" the professor slyly grinned.

"The Bible says that in God's eyes one day is like a thousand years."

"So, God created the world in 6,000 years?" he laughed.

"The thousand years to one day is a metaphor," I needlessly explained, "One day can mean a long, long time."

"So, you think the Bible is a metaphor. I thought Christians believed it literally," the gray-bearded professor quizzed me.

"Yes," I said with a coy bipolar blink and nod, "The Bible uses some metaphors to demonstrate the literal truth."

"So, you don't know the full truth," the professor quipped, setting a trap.

"How could I? We're talking about the truth and wisdom of an omnipotent, omniscient, ever-present, eternal God. It's like Mike Huckabee said, I'm not expected to know all of that. If I did, I wouldn't *need* God. I would *be* God."

"So, you believe in what you cannot know."

"That's right!" I exulted. "Just like you."

"What does that mean?"

"Can you prove that there is no God?" I said, seizing my chance to quiz the professor.

"No." He admitted quickly – to my surprise and glee.

"So, you <u>believe</u> that there is no God without <u>knowing</u> that there is no God."

He looked at me and shook his head. We were both fired-up with this battle and both enjoying the hard fun of challenging each other's wit.

"You see," I said, smiling upon my return to genius mode, "I think it takes as much faith for you to believe that there is no God as it does for me to believe that there is a God."

"I might agree with that," half-confessed the professor, "But my faith is based on evidence."

"So is mine," I firmly boasted, bright-eyed and a little too pleased with myself at what I assumed to be the professor's surprise.

"What evidence do you have that God exists," the professor demanded.

"I have eyewitness testimony."

"Yeah, uh-huh, what're you talking about?" The professor smirked, apparently miffed.

"The Gospels."

"C'mon, man. Those are two-thousand years old. What proof is there that they are real? Who wrote them?"

"Matthew, Mark, Luke, and John."

"And why should we believe them?"

The professor was asking legitimate questions. He wanted me to back up the truth of the Bible without referring to what the Bible says of itself. There is nothing out-of-line about that. Why should an unbeliever accept the Bible as true simply because the Bible states that it is true? Why should *I* believe that the Bible is the Word of God based only on the fact that it says it is the Word of God?

"Matthew and John were apostles of Christ. They knew Him personally. They saw Him and spoke with him after He rose from the dead. Mark and Luke knew the apostles."

"I've got a few problems with that," said the professor.

I wasn't exactly shocked. One sort of expects an atheist to have some trouble with a man asserting the Gospels to be fact.

"I'm not trying to prove this to you," I said.

"Sure you are," the professor flashed, "We're both trying to prove our positions to the other."

He was obviously right about that and we both knew it.

"You said that my faith is blind, not based on evidence. I'm giving you the evidence for what I believe. And, yeah, maybe I am trying to prove it to you," I confessed, knowing that it was more than just a maybe. At the very least, I wanted him to come away doubting his own position.

"Well, I've got a few problems with your Gospels. First, what makes you think they were telling the truth?"

"They had no reason to lie," I shot back rapid-fire. "What did they have to gain by lying? The leaders of the Romans and the Jews had crucified Christ. There was no great market for coming out and saying that He was alive. It wasn't going to make the apostles rich and famous. They were risking their lives by saying that Jesus rose from the dead – just like He had promised." [They were saying that the leaders of the Romans and Jews were wrong about something that was so important to them that they had killed for it.] (Strobel, 1998, pp.45,48)

The professor was not so easily impressed. "So, they wanted to stand up for what their leader had promised. What's so unusual about that?"

"Would you say something that you knew to be a lie if the only thing that it promised you – in this life – was persecution and maybe the death penalty?" (Strobel, 1998, pp.45,48)

"They didn't lie. They believed it," the professor winked, "Having a masters in psychology, you know that it is possible to believe something so much that you actually believe that you see a vision of it."

"Yes, that is true. But these men said that they were all together and saw him at the same time – together – a number of times. They said they ate with Him as a group – after He rose from the dead. And there is no record in the history of psychology of an identical mass hallucination." (Strobel, 1998, pp.238-240)

The professor was not impressed.

"You've heard of Jim Jones and his followers in Guyana? Hundreds of them drank the Kool-Aid and committed suicide because they believed in him."

"They did not have a mass hallucination. They were delusional, yes. They believed in Jim Jones, that he was some kind of messiah or god. But they did not all see identical visions – hallucinations – at the same time. They had the same distorted thinking, but it was not a mass hallucination. They did not all see the same thing – that wasn't really there – at the same time."

"When you believe something so strongly, it can cause you to see things that aren't there," the professor argued.

"Are you saying that the apostles and disciples, when they saw the risen Jesus, had the only mass hallucinations in all of history? And they had them together, identically, not once, but a number of times?"

The professor paused. He shook his gray head, rolled his eyes, and sighed as if I were nuts.

"So . . . you believe in levitation," mused the professor.

"What?"

The professor slowly raised his hands into the air, wiggling his fingers. "You believe that Jesus just one day floated up from the earth and went up into heaven?" the professor smiled crazily, rolling his eyes, and reminding me a bit of myself in genius mode.

"The Ascension," I asserted as though it were not so unusual. "Yes, I believe that Jesus ascended into heaven. I also believe that He is coming back the same way."

"And you're an educated man," the professor blinked in disbelief.

I shrugged and grinned bipolar.

"How can you believe that he levitated, just floated up to heaven?"

"He was God," I said with a flick of the wrist, still grinning.

"Oh, right. I forgot."

I questioned the professor. "Are you saying that He could not have ascended into heaven because it is impossible?"

"It *defies* the laws of nature!" he shriekingly bellowed.

"If Jesus were God, He would be able to do what is impossible for man – even levitate into heaven.

"If there was a God – a big if – He could do what is impossible for man to do," the professor admitted. Sort of.

"So, saying that it is impossible for man to levitate into heaven, is not proof that Jesus did not do it. It would be possible for Him. It would be easy for Him."

The professor shook his gray head once again. "If . . . He . . . were God."

"Well, that's some of the evidence for my faith. Not to mention the holes in the *theory* of evolution."

"Aw, no. Holes in evolution?" he groaned with that look I've come to know as saying, "You're crazy, but it's entertaining so I'll listen."

"You know, it is just a theory," I said.

[Many scientists do NOT believe it." (Hatfield, quoted in Strobel, 2004, p.31) **And even Darwin had his doubts.** [(Darwin, 1859, quoted in Strobel, 2004, pp.55-56) (Wells, Ph.D., quoted in Strobel, 2004, p.43)]

Somehow, the professor still was not convinced. "Darwin believed that his *theory* would be proven true," the professor punched back. "There are many, *many*, scientists who DO believe evolution.

"Well, let me give you an example." I paused. "Would you say that today's dogs evolved from wolves?" I asked, knowing full-well that the professor knew that I already knew his answer.

"Yes," he sighed with an obligatory smirk.

"And it wasn't as if one day a particular wolf gave birth to a fully evolved present-day dog."

"No. You don't understand evolution," he snapped, a little impatiently. "Through survival of the fittest and natural selection – over millions of years

– thousands of genetic mutations – over millions of years the wolf evolved to a dog."

"So, where are all those animals – mutations – between the wolf and the dog?"

The professor shook his head and cringed. He nearly shrieked, "They're dead!"

I took the professor's tone to mean that he thought that I might be an idiot – or, at least, impersonating an idiot for the sake of his irritation.

"No!" I pounced. "They're not just dead. They're extinct! Those categories of animals *don't exist anymore!*"

"So," he said, wincing and rapidly shaking his head in a short burst, "what's your point!?"

"My point is that they didn't survive."

"So what," his voice rose, "Some evolutions survive. Some don't."

"We still have wolves and we still have dogs, but all those thousands of evolutions in between – <u>they</u> did NOT survive.

"I don't think you understand evolution," he said.

"I'm not trying to disprove it."

"Sure you are."

"I said there were holes in the theory. The dog-wolf thing seems like a hole. Why didn't the alleged animals in-between survive?

We agreed to respectfully disagree and the professor was off to a chess match with his three companions.

As we parted, I said a wry "God bless you."

The professor did not laugh.

Judge for yourself where this next trek into bipolar boldness lands on the Ya'Zhynka Passive-Assertive-Aggressive scale.

The attorney who opposed me in my lawsuit against St. Thomas University School of Law had filed a motion which he titled, "DEFENDANTS' MOTION TO COMPEL PRO SE PLAINTIFF (that's me) TO CONDUCT HIMSELF IN A PROFESSIONAL MANNER. In his Motion, the attorney (hereinafter referred to by the pseudonym "Mr. Lester Scroop," "Mr. Scroop," "Scroop," or "Lester") complained that I had sent him a letter containing the following statement:

> *"Since my Christian faith is an issue in this case I thought I might make you aware of an upcoming movie and a current New York Times best-seller which are significant statements about Christianity. The book is "The Purpose-Driven Life" by Rick Warren. It was #1 on the best-seller list. The movie, which is being released next week is titled, "The Passion of the Christ.*
>
> *"Of course, I don't know anything regarding your beliefs about God. You may have long ago accepted Jesus as your Lord and Savior. In which case, I'm probably telling you things you already know."*

Seeing that Mr. Scroop was so troubled that he felt the need to make accusations against me with the Federal Court, I chose to give him a telephone call to see if we could "clear things up." Here is a non-verbatim summary of the gist of the conversation:

"Hello, this is attorney Les Scroop. How can I help you?"

"Hello, Mr. Scroop. This is Rich Jarzynka."

"Hello, Mr. Jarzynka," said Scroop with what I imagined to be a forced politeness, "How can I help you?"

I was surprised by the cordiality of his tone upon hearing that it was me on the other end of the line. Surely, he knew why I was calling and that I could not have been pleased with his accusatory Motion. I took a breath to re-set my frame of reference and pressed on with my agenda.

"I just received your Motion to Compel Me to Conduct Myself in a Professional Manner–

"Yes," Scroop interrupted with a hint of anticipation.

" . . . and I wanted to find out what I did that got under your skin so much," I said a little more directly than planned.

That did not go over so well with Scroop. "You sent me an irrelevant letter about my faith which has nothing to do with this case," he barked.

I paused, a little taken back by his sudden change of tone, and grinned nervously. "Mr Scroop –

"My faith has nothing to do with this case," he interrupted. Again. (I am working on it, but I still need to get better at dealing with being interrupted in mid-sentence.)

"Mr. Scroop," I began again, this time with just a little more intensity, "I was simply responding to your Written Interrogatory and Request for Production of Documents," I jabbed as my grin turned fiendish.

"That was not a response to my request. It was irrelevant," Scroop protested.

I pounced, knowing that the full weight of the evidence was four-square in my favor on this count.

"You sent a Request for Production of Documents, Mr. Scroop," I firmly baritoned. "And that Request demanded 'All documents which relate to Plaintiff's religious mission or divine mission, including religious texts, journal entries, literature, and correspondence.' You asked for those documents, Mr. Scroop, and now you're complaining about me sending them."

Mr. Scroop was silent. That sometimes happens when one gets hit with their own words. But I wasn't finished.

"And, Mr. Scroop, you also sent me an Interrogatory," I piled on. "And in that Interrogatory you asked, 'Do you believe you had a religious or divine mission during your attendance at St. Thomas University, and if so, describe the nature, objectives, foundations, authority, and circumstances related to such mission(s).' You asked about my faith."

"Mr. Jarzynka, your letter was irrelevant," boldly insisted Mr. Scroop.

"You asked about my faith," I boomed slowly, "and I responded. I sent you a letter about my faith. I told you that the book 'The Purpose Driven Life' had influenced my faith and that I had seen the movie, 'The Passion of the Christ,' on the recommendation of my church."

Attorney Lester Scroop was not satisfied. "You wrote in your letter that you don't know what my faith is. My faith has nothing to do with this case, Mr. Jarzynka."

I was more than ready for Lester's last comment and I let loose. "Mr. Scroop, <u>nobody's</u> faith has anything to do with this case. <u>You</u>, Mr. Scroop, made it a part of this case when you sent your Interrogatory and a request for all documents regarding <u>my</u> faith. If you want to know about my faith, I suggest that you read 'The Purpose Driven Life' and see 'The Passion of the Christ.'"

"I'm not going to spend my client's time reading a book and seeing a movie."

"Then why did you request that information?" I snapped.

Scroop quickly cracked back, "You said that you were on a mission from God to save the soul of a law professor."

"Mr Scroop, I am a child of God!" I growled, "And when you come after me because of my faith in Him, you come after Him."

"Nobody is coming after you because of your faith," Scroop said, sounding a little more softly combative.

"*Yes you are!*" I rapidly demanded, and the action briefly paused.

Mr. Scroop changed the subject and went lawyerly on to tell me that if I was unhappy with his Motion that I should write a Response and file it with the Court.

"O-o-o-h, I will be writing a Response," I cheerily warned Mr. Scroop, "You can count on that. And I won't need any extensions of time to get it done."

Mr. Scroop had repeatedly requested that the Court's deadlines be extended for *his* filings and he sounded like he was stung by my last remark.

"Well, while I've got you on the phone," Mr. Scroop snapped, "I should let you know that I will be scheduling your deposition."

It sounded to me like Mr. Scroop had just come up with the deposition idea on the spur of the moment as a counter-attack to my "extension of time" comment. I let him know that I would be pleased to appear for the deposition and asked, "When should I be expecting a check from you for the airfare, motel, and travel expenses?"

A picture flashed in my brain from twelve-hundred miles south – Scroop hitting the roof of his Florida office. He 'firmly' insisted that his client would not be paying my expenses and I 'firmly' mused, "Then . . . *you* . . .won't be taking my deposition."

Mr. Scroop persisted, demanding that he would, indeed, be taking my deposition in his office at the date and time of his choosing.

I didn't see any need to back down and by this time I was finding the whole thing fairly amusing, "Mr. Scroop, if you want to take my deposition," I cracked, half-singing, "you can either have your client pay my expenses or you can fly to Pittsburgh, but I am not spending my money so you can have your deposition."

"You chose to file this case in the Southern District of Florida," said Mr. Scroop.

"I filed this case in the Western District of Pennsylvania," I shot back, "Your predecessor filed a Motion to Dismiss for Improper Venue and the case was transferred to Florida," I said, now barking. "If you want to take the deposition, you'll do it here."

Scroop was not impressed. "That's not the way it works," said he.

"That's the way it's gonna work this time," said I.

"I'm scheduling your deposition," Scroop punched.

"And I'll be filing a Motion for a Protective Order."

Mr. Scroop then suggested that I stop wasting my money on a case that I could not possibly win and the conversation ended shortly thereafter and abruptly. I did not think fast enough to ask how much of his client's money he had "spent."

Mr. Scroop, true to his word, did, indeed, send me a letter to schedule the deposition. And I honored my commitment to file a Motion for Protective Order. The Court ruled that if Mr. Scroop wanted to take my deposition in Miami, his client, St. Thomas University, would have to pay half of my estimated travel expenses. I considered that a victory.

For reasons never made clear to me, Mr. Scroop was replaced on my case by another attorney from within the firm that he worked for. By the time the new attorney scheduled my deposition, the time limit set by the Court had expired. I filed an objection based on that fact and the Court ruled that the attorney was barred from taking my deposition. His firm did not finish the case. For some reason, I found that amusing.

I cannot imagine that anyone would think that either Mr. Scroop or I was passive during this discussion. And if the text reads as *"assertive,"* I would remind you that the written word does not quite convey the exact tone and volume of our voices.

The Court dealt with Mr. Scroop's Motion regarding my conduct by telling us both to behave ourselves. Another victory, I figured.

I am not about to give up my Bipolar Boldness. It has prevented me from being passively plowed over and it has taught me to stand up and speak out for the things that matter. However, as indicated above, I have yet to perfect my assertiveness. But God is at work.

"It is <u>not</u> by thinking that we cease to wonder at the (the world) . . . This world after all our science and sciences, is still a miracle; wonderful, inscrutable, magical and more, to whosoever will <u>think</u> of it."

- Thomas Carlyle (p.14-15)
(in <u>Tozer</u>, 1961)

CHAPTER 28

GOD LIKES THE CRAZY PEOPLE

"Rich-ieee!" the gleaming Caribbean, 30 year-old, ex-addict sings my name as the worship music soars and pounds to start the service. We embrace and I can feel the crazy coming off of him. We stand back and I look wildly into his wild-eyed grin, yelping, "Yeah! God likes the crazy people!" And he yelps back, "Rich-ieee! Because we'll get crazy for him!" And I let out a cackling howl as the music blares.

This man knows something about "crazy." He decided to get clean only after a drug deal got him thrown into the trunk of a car; driven into a field in Middle-of-Nowhere, New York; beaten, broken, bloodied, and left for dead until a woman – who just happened to be a Christian – came to the rescue. He is now every bit as rabid and raving for Christ as he ever was for crack-cocaine.

My Caribbean brother and I rejoice that God has so equipped us to get crazy for Him.

What am I getting at here? Well, my God has a long history of doing things that cause the world to shake its head and cry out, "Madness!" And sometimes He uses a willing wing-nut to carry out His mind-blowing plans.

Now, let me be clear. When I talk about "getting crazy for God," I am not talking about doing something stupid like taking a leap off of a third-story ledge to prove that God will send His angels to bear you up lest you dash your foot against a stone. Satan failed miserably when he tried to tempt Jesus with that perversion of scripture. God is not going to ask you to do something stupid, suicidal, or needlessly harmful. He does not need you to handle snakes or drink poison to prove that he is God.

However, God does sometimes call us to do things that seem to set the world ill-at-ease; praying in public, telling a stranger in a bar that Jesus rose from the dead and lives today, speaking out against gay marriage, lifting your hands in worship when the rest of the church is sitting on theirs, firmly but gently confronting a brother's false doctrine.

We crazy people are already familiar with the world's response to that which it deems not quite normal. Therefore, we might have a small advantage when called to some oddball mission. I'm not bragging. It's just the natural, logical consequences of our rollicking cyclothymia.

Consider God's mad history. Think of the many biblical characters who did great things at the Lord's command. How "normal" did they look in the eyes of the world?

Noah built an ark before the world had ever seen rain.

Abraham believed that his wife would conceive a child at the age of 90 and *reasoned* that God could – and would – raise the dead. And that was a couple of thousand years before Jesus proved it.

Moses went to Pharaoh and demanded, "Let my people go" – because a burning bush told him to do it. I have bipolar disorder, so, I don't always seem "normal," but I have never followed the orders of a shrub.

David, a little boy, took on Goliath. Think of a 14 year-old kid taking the football field, lining up against Baltimore Raven linebacker Ray Lewis or Steeler James Harrison, and telling him that he is going to hand him his head. That's nuts! But on the scale of craziness it measures a little shy of what David believed he could do when he teamed up with God. Ray Lewis is a hall-of-fame-type linebacker, but he is not 9 feet tall.

John the Baptist lived in the desert, eating locusts, wearing camel's hair, and telling Scribes and Pharisees to repent. Sounds a little crazy, doesn't it? Of course, that *did* get The Baptizer his head handed to him – literally. There was, however, none born of women who was greater than John. (Matthew 11:11) Why? Because he was anointed by God and followed God's command to do what looked crazy to the world.

Paul went out and told the world that he had been taken up into the third heaven where God revealed to him unspeakable mysteries. He ended up writing much of the New Testament. (Yes, from prison. He suffered much for looking and sounding crazy.) And he is still reaching the world for Christ. Being willing to look crazy was a good deal for him – even though it landed him shipwrecked, whipped and beaten, and sent to prison.

And get a load of this rarely quoted gem about Jesus:

> "When Jesus family heard what He was doing, they thought that He was crazy and went to get Him under control." (Mark 3:21, CEV)

We who have bipolar disorder are being prepared to do great things for God. We can praise wildly, witness boldly, pray publicly out loud, touch 'lepers' in their pain, and carry Christ where the faint of heart dare not go – without concern for what others might think. Because, for better and worse, we have previously been more than willing to be thought crazy for far less rational purposes.

We have screamed at the top of our lungs, broken down doors, run into traffic, fought with police, risked our lives giddily in the most deadly of neighborhoods, challenged giants, built arks of grand delusions, and eaten worse than locusts – all for foolish and even criminal purposes. How much more can we do for God – no matter how crazy in the eyes of the world?

Drug addicts become ministers. Former drunks witness on city streets and serve the homeless. Convicted felons fight to win souls. And a seven-time psych-warder writes a book blessing bipolar disorder.

"God likes the crazy people, Rich-ieee! Because we'll get crazy for Him!"

The Lord has used your disorder, your madness, to prepare you. Now, go in peace and get crazy for God. You were made for it!

(**WARNING:** *This does not give anybody who has bipolar disorder free reign to run wild without regard to the law, one's own safety, or the well-being of others. Getting crazy for God does have its limits.*)

CHAPTER 29

A ONE-MAN DEBATE

I once heard a professor describe bipolar disorder as "a more intense experience of reality." That hits home with me better than any other description. Manic-depressive thoughts and emotions are off-the-scale strong, but they are not unreal. They are a genuine response to the world and they are entwined with the social realities that we each experience and construct daily. In short, my bipolar emotions – as wild as they may sometimes be – are <u>not</u> a psychotic delusion.

Bipolar emotions, because they are intense, legitimate, and honest responses to the world, can help to reveal some more genuine understanding of human experience. Maybe we could consider bipolar living as "real-life magnified." Instead of taking 'normal' life and looking at it under a microscope, the person who has bipolar disorder blows it up ten times its actual size and lives it out large before the naked eye for all to see.

Yes, I do appreciate what my bipolar emotions have taught me. But I do *not* believe that we, as individuals or as a nation, should make important decisions based upon our feelings. The stakes are too high to let our sound judgment be overwhelmed with tides of emotion – especially rampant, mood-swingingly bipolar emotion. I do greatly value emotion and believe it can beneficially inform our reason, but, alas, I have dragged to the conclusion that it cannot dominate.

The strange value of bipolar for me is that, depending upon the then-current state of my wide-ranging emotions, I can get fairly worked-up on either side of an issue at different times. For instance, just yesterday (June 25, 2008) The United States Supreme Court ruled that it is 'cruel and unusual punishment' in violation of the Eighth Amendment to give the death penalty to a person guilty of raping a child. Most people have pretty strong opinions, one way or the other, about this decision. I have both.

When I hear about somebody raping a child, I want to choke the life out of the creature with my own hands. In fact, just writing this I can feel his throat in my hands as my thumbs crush his Adam's apple. A less-than-Christlike thought. But, nonetheless, a capacity that I don't mind having within my nature – just in case.

Now, here's the rub. Even as I was writing the above violent phrases, I thought, "Crushing a man's Adam's apple?! That would make me a murderer

– even if that man had raped a child. Wouldn't that make me, at least, a little like him?"

Whoa. That's a tough thought to have about yourself. I mean, I was getting into that image of the throat in the palms as the thumbs crushed the bones. I don't want, in any part, to be anything at all like a child rapist. But when I hear about a child being raped, I do want to strangle the guy. My emotions get wound up on both sides of this horror. I am righteously incensed to the point of wanting to strangle the guy, but I don't want to become a murderous thug. (Self-defense is an entirely other matter. Crush them bones.)

If I am in an agitated bipolar-nasty-mood depression, yeah, I want the guy to be strangled – not a kindly lethal injection, strangled! If I'm in a semi-elated, halfway realistic hypomania, then I say, "No, he is not a monster. What he did was monstrous – but he is still a human life."

So, the bipolar emotion gets me _thinking_ about arguments on both sides of the issue. Eventually, I can let the strong _feelings_ inform my reason without dominating it. (It might be wise for the person with bipolar not to rush into any important decisions. Let the emotion simmer and cool a little.)

But I still have not answered the question. My emotions have put me on both sides of the issue and forced me to either take a deeper look or pretend that the dilemma does not exist. But I have not been given a spirit of timidity (2Timothy 1:7), so, the question persists. How do I resolve the issue of whether some crimes should be punishable by death?

Well, I am a Christian. Matters of life and death clearly mandate heavy reliance on the Word of God. Uh-oh.

I know instantly that the Bible is not going to give an immediately apparent, definitive answer to the death penalty question. God, Himself, appears to be bipolar on the issue. The Bible has statements that seemingly support both sides. But, as Christians, we know that the Bible is internally consistent and that God never contradicts Himself. So, the non-Christian is perfectly justified in challenging me to face the contrasts in the following death penalty verses:

"Anyone who strikes a man and kills him shall surely be put to death." (Exodus 21:12)

"You must purge the evil from among you. The rest of the people will hear of this and be afraid, and never again will such an evil thing be done among you. Show no pity: life for life, eye for eye, tooth for tooth, hand for hand, foot for foot." (Deuteronomy 19:19b-21)

"If a man strikes someone with an iron object so that he dies, he is a murderer; the murderer shall be put to death . . . The avenger of blood shall put the murderer to death; when he meets him he shall put him to death." (Numbers 35:16,19)

"The wages of sin is death . . ." (Romans 6:23)

"Without the shedding of blood there is no forgiveness of sins." (Hebrews 9:22b)

"Whoever sheds the blood of man, by man shall his blood be shed; for in the image of God has God made man." (Genesis 9:6)

"For if you forgive men when they sin, your heavenly Father will also forgive you. But if you do not forgive men their sins, your Father will not forgive your sins." (Matthew 6:14-15)

"If any one of you is without sin, let him be the first to throw a stone at her." (John 8:7)

"(W)e have been made holy through the sacrifice of the body of Jesus Christ once for all." (Hebrews 10:10b)

"Do not judge, and you will not be judged. Do not condemn, and you will not be condemned. Forgive, and you will be forgiven." (Luke 6:37)

"Then Peter came to Jesus and asked, 'Lord how many times shall I forgive my brother when he sins against me? Up to seven times?"

> "Jesus answered, 'I tell you, not seven times, but seventy-seven times." (Matthew 18: 21-22)
>
> "You have heard that it was said to the people long ago, 'Do not murder, and anyone who murders will be subject to judgment.' But I tell you that anyone who is angry with his brother will be subject to judgment . . . (A)nyone who says, 'You fool!' will be in danger of the fire of hell." (Matthew 5:21,22a,c)
>
> "For whoever keeps the whole law and yet stumbles at just one point is guilty of breaking all of it." (James 2:10)

As I suspected, scripture does not render an immediately apparent, definitive answer to the question of capital punishment.

This task that I laid out for myself has not been an easy one. I admit that I came to this particular "one-man debate" with a strong bias *against* the use of the death penalty. (That might sound strange for somebody who calls himself a political conservative, but, let us never forget – bipolar. I occasionally do strange things.)

Despite my emotional reaction to want to choke the life out of a child rapist with my bare hands, I have long opposed the death penalty. However, in conducting this 'debate,' I saw an argument in favor of the death penalty that cited the scripture passage, "Whoever sheds the blood of man, by man shall his blood be shed." (Hanegraaff, 2004, pp.117-118) That challenged me to re-think my pre-suppositions and biases. And it has been a struggle.

This short chapter has taken far longer to write than I had anticipated. I procrastinated because I knew it would be difficult. I discovered that the one-man debate which I thought had been settled, was still underway even as I wrote. I put it off so much that, at the moment of this typing, every other chapter of this book has been completed and awaits my editing. It's time to get it done.

I can state the competing positions of this debate with the following scripture passages: "Whoever sheds the blood of man, by man shall his blood be shed" (Genesis 9:6) versus "Say to them, 'As surely as I live, declares the Sovereign Lord, I take no pleasure in the death of the wicked, but rather that they turn from their ways and live.'" (Ezekiel 33:11a)

Let me say right up front that I agree with those who contend that the Bible does support the use of the death penalty. I have no argument against the fact that God does mandate that the penalty for murder is death. How much clearer could He be than, "Whoever sheds the blood of man, by man shall his blood be shed?"

Of course, I am still troubled by the many verses that undeniably command us to forgive even as our heavenly Father has forgiven us.

Certainly, the non-Christian has a legitimate argument if he says, "Look, you can't have it both ways, Either you string the guy up by his neck until dead or you forgive him." And I can't complain. That is the bind in which I have willingly placed myself by taking on this debate from a biblical perspective. Which of God's laws should I ignore, the command to put the murderer to death or the command to forgive?

Three verses have released me from my bind:

"The wages of sin is death . . ." (Romans 6:23a)

"All have sinned and fallen short of the glory of God." (Romans 3:23)

And,

"If any one of you is without sin, let him be the first to throw a stone at her." (John 8:7)

Yes, God does command that the murderer be put to death. But He doesn't stop there. God commands that we all be put to death. He unflinchingly states, "The wages of sin is death." I do not read any qualifications there. It does not say that the wages of "murder and rape" is death. The penalty for _all_ sin is death.

That news is beyond bad for each and every one of us. Why? Because God also lays it out right between the eyes that, "_All_ have sinned and fallen short of the glory of God."

If we have _all_ sinned and the wages of _all_ sin is death, then we _all_ deserve the death penalty.

So, why were we not all struck dead at the moment of our first sin? Did God contradict Himself? Did He deny His own commandment? Did He change His mind about the penalty for _all_ sin being death?

Answer: No. No. And, no.

God sent His only begotten Son to live a perfect and sinless life of pure love and then go to the Cross to pay the death penalty for us. Our death penalty has already been paid. The death penalty that we still deserve. "While we were still sinners, Christ died for us." (Romans 5:8)

Of course, the wages of sin is still death and we all do still die a physical death. But "the gift of God is eternal life through Christ Jesus our Lord." (Romans 6:23b) We who surrender our lives to Christ, who paid the penalty that we deserve, will have eternal life with Him in paradise. When we embrace His Cross, the "death penalty" becomes an absurd oxymoron. For us, death is more a beginning than an end.

So, what about the death penalty for the unrepentant convicted murderer? Yes, God does mandate it. He means what He says when He says, "Whoever sheds the blood of man, by man shall his blood be shed." But He also means what He says when He says, "Let Him who is without sin cast the first stone." The murderer deserves to be strung up, but none of us is worthy to tie the noose and pull the trap door.

The Bible's death penalty verses are consistent with each other. God does, indeed, command that the murderer be put to death – by Someone who is without sin. That ain't you and it sure as shootin' ain't me.

Our courts get the death penalty correct – in a misguided way – when they impose the sentence and then allow the murderer to remain on death row until the One Who Is Without Sin decides to execute the sentence in the time and manner of His choosing. And while the murderer is on death row, God gives him the opportunity to repent and come to Christ. For He takes no pleasure in the death of the wicked, but rather that they turn from their ways and live. (Ezekiel 33:11a)

Let us pray that all who are on death row will come to repentance and give their lives to Christ. Let us pray that we will see them in heaven.

There are Christians who support the death penalty who will say that I am all wrong about this. I appreciate and respect their position. They have forced me not to accept an easy, emotion-based, answer to this question.

Christians who support the death penalty might argue that scripture specifically singles out murder as a sin for which God commands that the offender's blood must be shed *by men*. That He will not wait for the murderer to die a "natural" death. And I will ask, "Was not Christ's blood shed by *men*? And was his crucifixion not sufficient to pay the death penalty for *all* sin?

I would also point out to Christian supporters of the death penalty the occasions when God, Himself, unequivocally suspended the death penalty for two vicious murderers.

First, when Cain slew his brother, Abel, God said to Cain, ". . . (I)f anyone kills Cain, he will suffer vengeance seven times over." Then the Lord put a mark on Cain so that no one who found him would kill him. (Genesis 4:15) Cain had been found guilty of murder by God. Yet, God did not demand the death penalty for Cain. In fact, God ensured that no man would shed Cain's blood.

The second instance of God suspending a well-earned death penalty occurred when King David confessed that he had murdered Bathsheba's husband, Uriah. According to the law of God, David deserved the death penalty. His blood was to be shed by man. However, God, instead, said to David through the prophet Nathan, "The Lord has taken away your sin. You are not going to die." (2 Samuel 12: 13b)

The wages of sin *is* death, but only He Who is Without Sin is worthy to cast the first stone. (Romans 6:23, John 8:7)

As I said above, I do appreciate and respect the position of Christians who support the death penalty. They do not do so for the sake of satisfying anger or carrying out vengeance. They support the death penalty for what I believe are noble – and even Godly– purposes. They believe that human life is sacred, created in the image and likeness of a Holy God. And they believe that by executing the one who has defiled and extinguished that sacred life, they honor all human life *and* the God in whose image we are created.

My only disagreement with Christians who support the death penalty regards the identity of the Executioner.

Could I be wrong? Except for the Bible quotes, every word of this book has at least a fraction of something wrong with it. I'm sure of that because I know well the author – and he has not yet been perfected.

Fortunately for me, the aim of this chapter has not been to come up with the Definitive Biblical Proclamation for All Time Regarding the Death Penalty. Rather, it has been to demonstrate the vigorous emotional and intellectual one-man debate that can be an ongoing blessing of bipolar disorder.

When it comes to important and difficult issues like the death penalty, abortion, war, and personal relationships, being able to feel the strong emotions on both sides can actually help to keep me from making rash assumptions and extreme judgments. My strong emotions, it is true, have often led me to be reckless. However, I now know that if I can slow down and allow my emotions to inform (not dominate) my reason, then bipolar can strangely bless me with a more thorough understanding of some heated and complex issues.

So, the moral of the story is? "Pay attention to what your emotions are telling you, but, for goodness sake, let your brain have the final say!" Why else would God have put it so close to your mouth?

CHAPTER 30

RACING THOUGHTS

When the bipolar brain cranks into hypomania, there ensues a one man brainstorming session. Even in the writing of this book there have been times when my pen could not keep up with what was flashing through my brain. At times, I have started out thinking that I would write two paragraphs and I stopped four pages later. Of course, some of it was rambling garbage, but even that kept my mind moving, and as long as my mind is moving – asking questions, playing, dreaming, ruminating, and running around – I can hit on something that works. I can use the symptom of racing thoughts to explore ideas I otherwise would not have had and who knows where that might lead.

For instance, I first thought of writing about my hospitalizations nearly twenty years ago. But I did not have a format that worked for me – or enough material. About 18 months ago I was motivated to write about my lawsuit, but I had trouble figuring out a way to put it all together in a way that made sense. One day, while thinking about how to write up the drama of my expulsion from law school and feeling playful, I began randomly listing some thoughts about bipolar – the energy it gives me, the joy of letting myself be goofy, the intensity, the understanding of the emotional troubles that others experience.

In no time I had a list of twenty ways that I had benefitted from bipolar. The thoughts kept coming and I kept writing. And I had an idea for a second book – a long list of all the good things about bipolar disorder.

And then the dam broke. While writing the list, I saw the two books come together under one theme – even the loss of the lawsuit was a blessing. And I had the format I had groped after intermittently for eighteen years. Short chapters that do not have to be rigidly connected to each other, but are held loosely together under the same theme. That has always been the way I write best.

The problem, however, was that I felt that if I were going to write a book, I would have to carry the same event or idea over long pages and everything would have to build logically and follow closely on what went before. Well, my mind doesn't work that way and the events did not all happen logically and sequentially. No book was going to get written if I tried to force my brain to function less efficiently than God designed it to function – racing and ruminating, random digressions and all.

Because I got excited with my racing thoughts, I realized the connection between so many of the blessings in my life – even getting expelled, quitting my football scholarship, and homesteading in the psych ward. I realized that God truly had been at work in all of it for my good. And that gave me a format and a theme – through the mad blessing of racing thoughts.

You can use your racing thoughts to your benefit, but you must maintain control of them. If not, you can end up doing much that you will regret. Racing thoughts can lead to impulsivity which is also a symptom of bipolar disorder. Put the two together without some time to first slow down, get clear-headed advice, and make scripturally-consistent decisions, and you have a recipe for disaster.

Impulsively taking drastic, unconsidered action on your racing thoughts can have agonizing long-term consequences; Giving away ALL of your money, jumping into bed with somebody not your spouse and making a baby, quitting your job and abandoning your home to walk across the country without a dollar in your pocket, deciding to tell the world that you are Jesus. And no matter how good and right it feels at the time, you Will crash.

It is important to recognize when your thoughts are racing. You do not want to get so wound up in them that you forget your responsibilities. When I am really cranked up with writing it is possible for me to lose all track of time. In itself, that is not a bad thing, but if it causes me to forget to pick up my mom from work or mow my old man's lawn, it can cause no small aggravation. After 46 years, my parents are not surprised by it. By about the third time, however, friends and employers find it less than a quirky charm.

Harness your racing thoughts. Use them like a brainstorming session to dream, entertain new ideas, and imagine some fascinating *possibilities*. But don't do anything drastic – without first slowing down, getting Godly advice from a wise and trustworthy friend, and making a scripturally consistent decision.

CHAPTER 31

BIPOLAR DIARY, MEDICATION

—⚅—

"*I still get ticked off about having to take medication. Putting chemicals into my body to change my brain is as distasteful an idea to me as it is to anyone else.*

"*Right now, it is 7:57 PM, June 17, 2006. I am sitting in the food court of Ross Park Mall in the North Hills of Pittsburgh and I have not woke-up all day. Yeah, I got out of bed at 9:00 AM, but I had a tremendous seroquel hangover and could hardly move all day. After breakfast and a cup of coffee, I lay on the couch and fell back asleep.*"

(I cannot explain how much I despise that med-hangover feeling. It is the dead opposite of the best of what hypo-manic bipolar mental and physical energy has to offer. Energized, but not unsafe. Ideas firing away, but not rambling incoherently. Excited, getting things done, taking action, but not recklessly impulsive. That is the place where I want to live.)

"This hangover – in the not too distant past – would have caused me to cut back on the seroquel without consulting my doctor. I'd be screaming, "He doesn't know a (curse) thing about how this (curse) makes me feel. I'm knocked out all day. How can I live like this?" But that is not going to happen today.

"In the middle of March 2006 – 3 months ago – I checked into WPIC (Western Psychiatric Institute and Clinic). Dr. Mullick adjusted my medication dosage while I was there. When I left I was prescribed 100mg. Zoloft, 400mg. seroquel, and 1750mg. of depakote. I have taken the prescribed dosage everyday since then and I am not about to stop now. Yes, I feel awful today. My head feels heavy and swollen. I'm dead tired. And I'm having trouble concentrating. I'm in a (curse) seroquel stupor. But the truth is that this is just one day and I haven't had any manic-depressive symptoms since I started taking 400mg. of seroquel 3 months ago. I will take it again tonight. It ticks me off, but I will take it."

I did keep taking the medication as prescribed and it continued to help alleviate my symptoms. But I eventually did tell Dr. Mullick that I wanted to stop taking seroquel and depakote because I was concerned about their possible long-term adverse effects and I hate the occasional hangover feeling; and I did not believe that depakote was effectively stabilizing my moods.

I have been in treatment with Dr. Mullick since 1996. He has learned that if I do not believe in a treatment, I will, at some point, refuse to comply with it. And he is very willing to provide alternatives. There are more than I had imagined. He suggested that I try lamictal as a mood stabilizer rather than taking only Zoloft (an anti-depressant) as I had insisted. We negotiated. He gave me some literature on lamictal. I agreed to read it and consider the possibility of using lamictal. Dr. Mullick agreed to prescribe me only Zoloft until my next appointment with him. I learned that lamictal is an antiseizure medication that is also used as a mood-stablilizer and helps to treat the depressive symptoms of bipolar. I have been taking it now for two years with greater success than ever.

Don't be afraid to disagree with your doctor and request alternative treatments. And be honest with him. Follow the treatment he has prescribed and tell him what you think is working and what is not. If you miss medication dosages or deliberately stop taking it, tell your doctor. Be honest about it. If you're not, your doctor won't know what is going on and he won't be able to adjust your treatment accordingly. He cannot effectively assess your symptoms and adjust your treatment if he thinks you are taking medications that you are not. He is there to work for you. You are free to negotiate your treatment with him and reject his suggestions if that is what you feel you must do. Just let him know what you are doing so he can make a well-informed assessment of your condition. Otherwise, you and he will have no way of knowing whether his suggestions for treatment make any sense at all.

Regarding the medication hangover feeling: I am NOT a doctor and I am absolutely NOT prescribing anything for anybody. I will only say that since starting to take vitamin B12, folic acid, and the amino acid glutamine one year ago, my hangover symptoms have been greatly reduced. If you having feelings of stupor or hangover from medications (feeling drowsy or like you cannot wake up) you may wish to tell your doctor about those symptoms and ask him about taking supplements. **WARNING!: Consult your doctor before trying any supplements on your own. They may interact harmfully with your condition, your medications, your specific diagnosis of bipolar disorder, your unique medical history, and/or your current health and illness status.** **Follow your doctor's recommendations regarding supplements. What works for me might KILL you. Talk to your doctor!**

*"You changed my mourning into dancing;
O, Lord, my God, forever will I give you thanks."*
　　　　Psalm 30: 13b (New American Bible)

CHAPTER 32

LOUSY vs. PSYCH-WARD LOUSY

When I feel lousy, I have past, exceedingly abundant lousier feelings to compare it to. (Yes, I know. It should read, ". . . with which to compare it," but this is not being submitted to the obsessive-compulsive, mad rigors of a law review editor.)

Of course, I have times when I still feel rotten. Medication, counseling, and the joy of the Lord do not mean eternally constant bliss. And though I do have a wonderful peace by the grace of God, I don't remember Him ever promising that I would never have another bad day. Indeed, today (May 17, 2008) is one.

I went to bed last night having joyfully eaten half-a-jar of peanuts and half-a-meal too much. It is not uncommon. But last night it didn't sit quite right in my belly and when I don't sleep well, I wake up bad. Bipolar disorder can often disturb a person's sleep.

So, now, whenever I have a bad night's sleep for any reason, I wake with a feeling similar to a semi-comatose and agitated bipolar morning. It ain't good. And it can make me wonder whether it is the beginning of a downward spiral. Far worse than "ain't good."

I woke at 5:30 (yes, A.M.) and lay wide-awake for an hour, still feeling the quease of my peanut near-binge. I sat at the edge of the bed, head down and eyes closed, wondering how stiff my legs and back might be when I stood. (I now can admit that working-out takes a greater toll now that I am not 26, or 35, or 40. I tell myself that it's mostly because I'm still capable of making the mistake of doing the workout of 15 years ago. Bipolar blessing and bipolar madness.) Slowly, I pulled myself halfway up, grunted, felt the cobwebs in my head, stalled, and straightened. I considered collapsing, but I knew I was not going to fall back asleep. I made my way down the steps, fixed a pot of coffee, and saw that it was one of those drizzly, 50 – degree, mind-numbingly, less-than-splendid days we can have in Pittsburgh right in the middle of May. Oh, how I wanted to sleep through the whole thing. Somebody scream at me!

"Fool! Stop your blasted weeping and moaning!"

Any day this side of the locked psych ward doors is a pretty darn good one.

CHAPTER 33

ACCEPTING GIFTS

I have never liked asking anyone to help me to do anything. Consequently, much was left undone, never begun, or screwed up to the point of having to be fixed by the person I failed to ask for help in the first place.

Part of the reason for my not asking for help was a timid desire not to inconvenience anybody – except, of course, my family. Them I was all too willing to inconvenience. But another, more nefarious, motivation was pride. "If I can't do it myself," I reasoned (or *un*reasoned), "then it isn't worth doing. I'm not going to put up with letting somebody else show me how to do this. I'm an idiot for not being able to do this." All of these excuses came down to pride. Who am I to think that I should be able to do everything for myself?

Bipolar disorder breaks pride. When you're so bound up from depression and medication that you need a nurse to give you an enema and then don't get to the commode on time, pride goeth before a fall. When the guilt of your sin incapacitates you to the point of hospitalization, you recognize that all your pride is false.

It is still difficult for me to ask for help. Even after a good, harsh breaking, pride does rear up. But, at least, I now view asking for help as an occasionally good thing that I want to learn to do better.

In the past, whenever somebody wanted to give me something that I could not afford to buy for myself, I felt like a "charity case." I would get angry about not being able to purchase it for myself. Now, I have a completely changed view about gifts and I am getting comfortable with it. I don't go out asking people to give me things I can't afford. I know that I already have everything I need and always will. But if somebody wants to give me something unsolicited, that is their choice and their desire. I don't deny them that.

Bob Dylan sang in <u>Forever Young</u> (1973), "May you always do for others and let others do for you." It's a beautiful line. Sometimes, when a person wants to give me something or do an act of kindness for me, it is my gift to them to be humble enough to let them help.

Over the years, because of bipolar, there have been numerous times when I have had little choice but to accept the help of others – no matter how much I despised myself for it. When a brain disorder leaves you flat on your back, out of work, raving and/or stupefied, you either let somebody help you (emotionally _and_ financially) or you land on the street. I was so fed up with myself that I did consider the street. Briefly. I instantly chose help. It's warmer and not so hungry. I guess my pride was breaking.

Those times when I was so mentally, emotionally, and physically incapable forced me to rely on the kindness of strangers – and family. (Blessedly, no family became strangers)

I battled long and fiercely against the idea, but I finally accepted the notion that it is impossible for me to be completely competent. And having to accept the help of others brought me a good deal closer to proudly declaring, "I can't do one blasted thing for myself. Every good thing I have, think, do, or say is a gift from God – and I don't deserve it."

So why did it take me eighteen years after my first psych ward stay to make that declaration? Pride is stubborn. Even now. So, if you ever hear me boast of anything other than Christ, be sure to remind me of that June 1988 enema and my failure to get to the commode.

Yes, indeed, in _all_ things God works for the good of those who love Him. (Romans 8:28)

And knocking me down a peg or two when I truly need it is a gift that I can accept.

CHAPTER 34

BIPOLAR, BUT SINGLE-HEARTED

In the spring of 1998, I publicly revealed that the orgasm is not the crowning achievement of my life.

Having been bombarded for months with the "spin" regarding Bill Clinton's most infamous national sex scandal, I felt compelled to make my own statement. I was sickened by the excuses. "It was just a lie about sex." "Everybody cheats." "Boys will be boys." "That depends on what the definition of the word 'is' is." And my favorite; "If I were Clinton, I'd have done it, too." To which I quickly responded, "And I wouldn't want you to be President, either."

I finally had enough. In a bipolar moment of manic grace, I wrote the following letter which was printed in the Pittsburgh Post-Gazette:

> *"I am a 35-year-old male and since the news of the Clinton sex crisis broke, I have been repulsed by the theory, 'So what? Every man cheats.'*
>
> *"Not only do I intend not to cheat if I ever marry, it is also my rock-solid conviction that the next time I have any type of "sexual relations" will be on my wedding night.*
>
> *"And if I never marry? That's right.*
>
> *"I am enjoying life, and abstinence has yet to do me any harm."*

I am single. I have been that way for over 46 years and I may well stay that way the rest of my life. I do not know what God's will is for my future regarding marriage, but I do know that for the first 46 years His will has been for me NOT to be married.

From my perspective as an outsider, marriage looks difficult. The Apostle Paul said that those who marry will face many troubles in this life. (1 Corinthians 7:28b) And couples, rich and poor, saved and unsaved, happy and troubled, have told me that marriage is hard work. Bipolar disorder would not make it any easier.

Bipolar disorder has made long-term relationships difficult for me. The emotions get extreme for even non-manic depressives when they are "in-love," but for me it is doubled, tripled, and more. It feels perfectly magnificent – and it is entirely unhinged from physical reality.

My emotions are not only extreme when it comes to anger, depression, agitation, and elation, I also love massively and intensely. I spend huge amounts of quality time, listening close to every word. I give crazy-big-honey-baby-bear hugs. I buy flowers, encourage, and take out the trash. I do crazy stuff like take my girlfriend on a spur-of-the-moment $550 hot air balloon ride, not knowing for sure how I will keep making the payments on my used Dodge 600 convertible and oft-deferred, never-ending school loans. It is fantasmaglorifically wonderful. Until it hurls all of my other emotions beyond passion and into madness.

I struggled with being single. I prayed for marriage. I asked God – many times – for a wife whom I could love as Jesus loves the Church. I longed to have kids. And as I moved into my late thirties, it hurt to think that I would "end up alone."

From the time I was in my mid-twenties, I sensed that I might be one of those apparently rare people whom God calls to the single life. I imagine it sounds strange to many people that God would actually call somebody to be, and remain, single. It seems that our culture believes that there are three types of people when it comes to marital status: married and happy; married and struggling; and single or divorced and yearning for "that special someone who will complete them." I am none of the above.

Singleness is not a disease, disorder, or failure. Paul had this to say about his own unmarried life: "I wish that all men were as I am. But each man has his own gift from God; one has this gift, another has that. Now to the unmarried and the widows I say: It is good for them to stay unmarried, as I am." (1

Corinthians 7: 6b – 8) Paul considered his singleness a gift!

I used to complain to God with grudging tolerance, "Alright! If you want me to be single, I'll deal with it. But I don't have to like it!"

Now, I embrace the single life. It is such a blessing that if I someday bump into a woman who is Godly "perfect" for me, it would be difficult for me to give up what I have now in exchange for marriage.

What is so good about the single life?

Solitude.

I am often alone, but I am *never* lonely. Never!

Solitude is my choice and I crave it. It is NOT loneliness. It is a time when I can be quiet and at-rest in my soul and spirit. It is a time when I can contemplate and meditate or become very active in my thoughts, emotions, and imagination. It is a time when I can simply dwell in the Presence of God without saying a word or pray and praise rambunctiously out loud and even hear from God. It is an amazing, dumbfounding, deep joy; an inspiring, miraculous and motivating wonder. I could not give up that kind of solitude for all the world. And because I am single, I can choose to go into that solitude as often as I like without any concern that I might be neglecting my wife and family.

I once heard a visiting pastor at Allison Park Church say, "Your ministry flows out of your communion." Solitude gives me the opportunity for that deep communion with God that reveals and creates ministry. And empowers me to push into whatever ministry God has for me.

And I am _never_ lonely.

The Declaration of Independence says that "all men are . . . endowed by (our) Creator with certain unalienable Rights (and) that among these" is Liberty. I am not saying that a married man cannot have Liberty, but there is no way that he can have it like I do. I do what I want, when I want, in the exact way that I want to do it. Almost.

Paul was speaking of the kind of freedom that I have when he wrote, "I would like you to be free from concern. An unmarried man is concerned about the Lord's affairs – how he can please the Lord. But a married man is concerned about the affairs of the world – how he can please his wife – and his interests are divided." (1 Corinthians 7: 32 – 34a)

Paul was not just saying this to pacify the lonely hearts clubs of his day and ours. An unmarried Christian man like me really is free for the affairs of the Lord. I can spend much time reading the Word of God and dwelling in His Presence. If I meet a person who is depressed and feels the need for a Christian friend, I am free to stay there. I don't have to be concerned about getting home to what is rightly a married man's first priority in Christ; being a Godly husband and father.

I am free to counsel, minister, pray, preach, and witness whenever God may call and wherever He may choose to send me. In contrast, a Lutheran minister with whom I previously worked, once heard from his wife that their pre-teen son had asked, "When do _We_ get to be Daddy's family?" He had to make some changes. He was a fully-ordained, well-trained minister with a masters degree in Divinity, but he did not have the same freedom to minister that I do.

Of course – I can also choose to lie on the couch and turn on the Pirates game with a full grease-bag of Wise sour cream and onion potato chips by my side. There, quite seriously, is a lot to be said for that. And I am *never* lonely.

I guess it is possible that I may someday marry. (Good-bye couch, Pirates, and potato chips) I am not searching and yearning for it, but who knows what God has planned. It might be time for Him to throw me a curve. (For me, it would probably be more like a knuckleball.) But I know that for the first 46 years of my life, God has called me to be single and He has empowered me to live that life as a blessing.

It is ironic and, maybe, paradoxical, but embracing the single life has, in some ways, made me more capable of being the husband God would want me to be. If I married now, I would not be placing upon my wife the burden of being expected to somehow complete me. I find my completion in Christ. Also, I would not now make the mistake of marrying simply because I am "in-love" or need to spare myself the pseudo-horror of "ending up alone."

If I married now, it would be because I had found a woman whom God had brought into my life; with whom I could truly be partners in going at the world together in a Godly way, according to God's will; living together in the intimacy of Christ; joined together in a shared mission and ministry;

knowing that God had called me to be the spiritual servant-leader of our marriage and to love my wife as Christ loves the Church – even when I can't stand her. We would have all the difficulties of every other marriage, but we would not be counting on our relationship to bring us our individual fulfillment.

I do believe that a person who has bipolar can have a good marriage, but the disorder is a factor to be thoroughly considered by _both_ parties before they commit the rest of their lives to each other. They will have unique challenges to face and I would recommend seeing a counselor together to start facing those challenges – _prior_ to making the final decision to be wed into each other for life.

The person with bipolar disorder must be open about it with his/her potential spouse. I'm not saying that it is first-date subject matter. But you do owe it to yourself and your potential spouse to make sure that they are fully informed about your condition and your unique symptoms. You and he/she need to have pre-conceived options for dealing with you at your worst. Most likely, she has not yet seen you at your worst. Be honest about it and come up with a strategy for dealing with a bipolar episode now – while you are at your best.

A few suggestions:

1. Allow your spouse the right – and even the responsibility or obligation – to respectfully tell you his/her observations regarding your behavior and moods. Believe it or not, if you have bipolar, you need someone who will assertively tell you

his/her honest observations of your mood and behavior – especially when it begins to change. Your spouse cannot be afraid to tell you what she sees happening with you. If you listen to her, you can check your symptoms for yourself and possibly head off a bipolar episode.

2. Tell your spouse ahead of time what to look for in a manic or depressed episode. Do you get exceptionally quiet or withdrawn as you go into a period of depression? Tell her ahead of time. Do you start to curse more when a period of manic irritability starts to hit? Tell her. Is it difficult to get to sleep, stay asleep, or wake up? Do you eat more or less? Do you lose interest in work, hobbies, or entertainment? Do you avoid people? Tell her – *ahead of time*. She can help. And she needs to know so she can find a way to deal with this stuff herself. The worst thing for a spouse is to not know what is causing the abrupt changes in your emotions and behavior.

3. Commit to seeing a counselor no less than once a month throughout your entire marriage. Make sure that during every appointment – before leaving – you schedule with the counselor your next appointment. Let your spouse know the date and time and KEEP THE APPOINTMENT. Even if from this day forward you never have another symptom, KEEP THE COUNSELING APPOINTMENTS. You may not have anything pertinent to discuss with the counselor, but it is worth doing for the sake of your spouse's peace of mind. (I have not had a significant symptom

in over two years, but I do keep seeing my counselor. And I don't have a spouse.) He/she will know that you are actively working to maintain your mental health and emotional stability and that you have not decided that you no longer have bipolar disorder. Further, when you have a continuing relationship with the same counselor, you can call him immediately if you get hit with an unexpected stressor or the normal ones get a little bigger than usual. Get to the counselor and deal with the problem before it shoves your marriage over a cliff.

4. Commit to taking whatever medications you have negotiated with your doctor. That does not mean that you are sentenced to taking the same medications in the same dosages for the rest of your life no matter the side effects. You should not have to live life in a stupor or be unable to function because the treatment is nearly as bad as the illness. Just commit that any changes will be made with the guidance of your doctor. Call your doctor and tell him your concerns. He works for *you*. Tell him that you want a change either in the type of medication or the dosage. If he refuses and does not give you a satisfactory reason, find another doctor. But don't change the medication dosage or stop taking it on your own – before you see the new doctor! Commit to your spouse that you will never change your medication regimen without the guidance of your doctor. And let your spouse speak with your doctor about your treatment. She is dealing

with bipolar disorder just as much as you are and she needs to know what to expect. Remember, she chose to allow bipolar into her life because she loves you. She could have avoided it. She deserves to know what is going on.
5. Let your spouse know that it will not be the end of the marriage if there comes a time when the symptoms of the disorder become too much for him/her to handle and he/she needs to take a break from you. Of course, your spouse also needs to commit to not ending the marriage because of your bipolar disorder. That should be expected – if you were open about the disorder with your spouse and he/she still chose to marry. Bipolar is a part of that "for better or worse, till death" stuff to which God has not yet called me.

That's one unmarried manic-depressive's advice for a bipolar marriage. Consider the source and take it for what it's worth.

I would consider it to be a tremendous blessing if God did someday call me to be married. But I know that the single life is also a tremendous blessing and that bipolar has not so much kept me from marriage as it has kept me in the holy calling of the single life. I could not recommend it any more highly and I have this word of support from the wisdom of Solomon:

"It is better to live in the corner of an attic than with a contentious wife in a lovely home." (Proverbs 25:24 New Living Translation)

I believe that Christ died for me because it is incredible;
I believe that He rose from the dead because it is impossible."
- A.W. Tozer, quoting an early church father (1961, p.19)

CHAPTER 35

COMFORTING WITH THE COMFORT GIVEN, Part II

I was not feeling as close to God as I often do and I knew that it was not His fault.

I had not turned my back on Him and I was not neck-deep in immorality. I was just not as disciplined in prayer and scripture as I had been. I missed a couple of services due to vacation and a broken ankle. And I realized that I had been blessing less, cussing more, and saying some downright mean things about people who might have had it coming – but it wasn't mine to give.

I returned home from visiting my sisters, brother-in-law, and nephews in Nashville and I was looking forward to getting back to Allison Park church. I whole-heartedly believed that being fully involved in a service there and praising God with my home church family would bring me back to where I needed to be with God.

I arrived at church just after the start of the Saturday night service. I usually get there a few minutes early to pray and dwell quietly in the presence of God before the music begins and rolls into the clapping, shouting, singing, and hand-raised hallelujahs that I love. Getting there a little late was a symptom of my recent drift. I wanted to be there, but no so much that I made the effort to show up on time.

I sang and prayed – and did so sincerely – but I just wasn't feeling it. Now I realize that I don't always need to have shivers up and down my spine to know that the Holy Spirit is with me, but this time I wanted to "feel" His presence.

One of the pastors got up and led the congregation in some intense prayer for a couple of members of the church who were in dire need. One of those we prayed for was a 34 year-old man named James. I had never heard of him. Before we began to pray the pastor told us that James had been in a serious car accident the previous Friday night. He had been unconscious since the time of the accident and was non-responsive. He was hospitalized in the neuro intensive care unit at Allegheny General Hospital. The same place my 14 year-old niece had been treated when she suffered a traumatic brain injury in a car accident nearly seven years earlier.

I was struck by the similarities between James' situation and that of my niece. I prayed for his healing and for his family, but soon forgot about him.

The service continued. I paid attention, but I was not overwhelmed. Two of the pastors preached about "making our lives count," getting to know God more," "bringing our loved ones to salvation," and "learning to hear and follow God's direction." All great stuff, but nothing had me especially "feeling" the intimate presence of God. (Again, we're not always going to feel Him with us and it is important to _know_ that He is with us when He "feels" far off, but this day I was hoping to feel His presence.)

At the end of the service, Pastor Jeff Leake called forward people who felt that they had been recently seeking the Lord's more specific direction, but were just not getting anywhere. That was not me. I was not seeking understanding about a relationship or wondering what to write next or trying to figure out whether I should go back to work. Considering the bipolar life, things have been straight-down-the-line and unconfused for me for the last twenty months. But, at Pastor Jeff's invitation, I joined in praying for those who were seeking direction. And, as I was praying for them, I asked God to speak to me.

Communion with God is more wonderful than any other earthly experience. But when you ask Him to speak to you, that does not obligate Him to tell you something you expect – or want – to hear. It does, however, obligate you to do what He says do. Ask anyway! Let Him know that you trust His love for you even if He is to call you into a time of struggle. He will be with you in it, loving you more than you can imagine and working for your absolute best.

The service ended and I sat in the front row and meditated. All very good, but nothing out of the ordinary.

I went back to Allison Park Church the following morning to sing praise at the end of the 9:00 service and the beginning of the 11:00 service. Pastor Jeff again called forward those who were seeking direction from God. I joined in the prayer and did much the same as the night before, but something started to stir between the 9:00 service and the beginning of the 11:00 service. And I was "feeling" God's presence as I had hoped the night before.

I caught the attention of Pastor James Leake, Jeff's father, who had preached with Jeff during the two services. I told him that I had been at both services and that with all of the prayer, praise, and seeking God that had already occurred, I was sensing that God might speak to people arriving for the 11:00 service even before the preaching began. He said that he believed that with all his heart and I sat down, hoping that somebody would get the direction they had been seeking.

Somebody did.

We sang and prayed and one of the pastors again prayed for James, the man who was hospitalized and unconscious at Allegheny General after a car accident. And I again thought of my niece, Samantha, and how she had lain in that same hospital, unconscious from a car accident for three or four days. How traumatized we all were, like somebody had slammed the brakes on time. And as I remembered the feeling that the world had stopped, God said, "Go."

"What? . . . Wait. I don't really want— But, I don't even know these people. I wanna get a snack and go to the gym."

I prayed fervently for James and we started into another worship song. And that shiver that I had been hoping for hit my neck, shoulders, and spine so strong that I visibly shook – and the Holy Spirit took control. Yes! God was doing it again. Shaking me up. Drawing me close. Using me! Hallelujah!

"Thank you, God. I'm going. Help."

Before I got to the outer door, the Holy Spirit more than whispered, "You fasted for Samantha."

"Yes, I did. 40 hours."

He did not have to say any more. I looked at the clock. 11:20AM. I was done eating until Tuesday morning.

I sang worship songs and prayed in tongues much of the way to the hospital. I needed to be empowered. I found the neuro intensive care unit's waiting room and started asking around for James' family. I had never before seen them or James. They were not there.

I searched through the empty halls and challenged myself not to leave. Eventually, I stumbled upon another waiting area near the intensive care unit. There were several groups of people scattered around the large room. I took a breath and nervously pushed myself forward to ask people if they were there for James. I felt like an intrusive and weird pain-in-the-butt, but I believed that God had sent me there and He gave me the courage to be the pain that I needed to be.

James' family was not in the second waiting room, either. I was discouraged and doubtful. "Maybe I got this wrong," I thought. "Maybe God did not send me here. It was all just in my head. Well, maybe he wanted me to come, but not to actually meet James' family." I considered leaving, but decided to wait.

As I sat there and the beautiful summer Sunday afternoon unfolded outside of the hospital, a married couple whom I vaguely recognized from another church entered the waiting room. The husband and I squinted toward each other with that foggy look that hesitates to say, "don't I know you from somewhere?" I said a tentative, "Hello," and he nodded, "St. Bonaventure, right?" They introduced themselves as Mario and Judy and one of them said astoundingly, "Are you here to see James?" I replied and before I could ask if they were his parents, they told me that his family might be in the cafeteria and asked if I wanted to walk there with them. I told them how and why I ended up at the hospital. And we agreed that God had sent me – and put us in each other's path.

Mario and Judy introduced me to James' family and any anxiety I had about speaking with them easily fell away. Suddenly, it did not seem so crazy to say to them that God had told me to visit them. God had opened all the doors to enable me to do what He had sent me to do. He made it easy for me to tell James' parents of my niece's car accident and brain injury and the healing God did for her in that very neuro intensive care unit.

I skeptically heard God's voice and hesitated to obey, and still He honored me with the blessing of comforting with the comfort I have been given.

"... [W]e might be wise to follow the insight of the enraptured heart rather than the more cautious reasonings of the theological mind."
> - A.W. Tozer

CHAPTER 36

NO END IN SIGHT

In the late 1980's and early 1990's, Bob Dylan did hundreds of seemingly constant worldwide concerts. He was always on tour. Not surprisingly, he titled his odyssey, "The Never-Ending Tour." When writing later about those concerts, Dylan stated, "by the way, don't be bewildered by the Never Ending Tour chatter. There was a Never Ending tour, but it ended in '91." (1993)

Bipolar Disorder is my Never-Ending Tour. Unlike Mr. Dylan's tour, however, my bipolar adventure, though it may change, will never truly end. To some, that will sound like a nightmare. For them, bipolar is – so far – nothing but agony. It is for them that I have attempted here to reveal blessing in the midst of that agony.

I have known intimately the mind-wrecking despair, anger, and agitation of manic-depression. So, all who have bipolar do have my empathy (not sympathy). But I refuse to be constrained to the narrow view of bipolar that reduces it to a collection of pathological symptoms. My experience has taught me that there is blessing in bipolar. I have it and I will continue to have it. I may even have it, one day, in heaven. Hallelujah! My Never-Ending Tour.

Bipolar disorder is a _part_ of who I am. It is a _part_ of my personality. It is _not_ my identity. I am far more than bipolar, but it does impact my thinking, feeling, living, moving, and having my being. Without bipolar disorder, I would still recognize myself, but I would not be quite the same. In fact, I might not like that man. I might find him boring.

If you have bipolar disorder, know that it will always be a unique adventure and possibly a blessing. If you give the adventure to Christ and bring it under His authority, it will be a rolling thunder shot of wonder. You will be awestruck by the simple, dumbfounded by your own words, stupefied with amazement, and redundant.

If you go at the bipolar life without Christ, it will still be an adventure. Something like being drafted into the jungles of Vietnam. It's up to you. Will bipolar be an adventure with God – or a tour of duty without Him? I have tried it both ways and I say, "Man, you've got bipolar! You're going into the jungle, either way. Take God with you!" But that's just one manic-depressive's not-so-humble opinion. Have it your way. There may be those who liked the Vietnam War and wish they could have stayed. There are also those, I suppose, who would choose to go to hell.

I want you to have the hope that I have found in, and through, bipolar. I want you to know that you can have joy. And I want you to know that there is blessing in having depression. Note that I did not say that blessing will come out of depression or that it will turn into a blessing. There is blessing in it right here and right now – beyond what I have written in the previous pages.

I will not minimize the agony you have suffered. I remember Abraham Biggs. But I am convinced that you can find blessings in bipolar just as wonderful as those that I have known. You may even find some that I don't know.

Nobody should be fool enough to choose to have depression or bipolar. It hurts. Bad! But if you do have it, you need to know that you can find good in it. It is valuable to you. And God will use it for your absolute best. (Romans 8:28) Believe that and He will make you see it – probably in unexpected ways.

So, how do you start finding your own blessings in bipolar?

1. Embrace Christ.

Yes, that is obvious. But I am not about to take it for granted. If you want to know the blessings of bipolar disorder, you must first accept the greatest blessing that God has for every one of us. His Son. Jesus lived a sinless life of pure love and willingly chose to be killed on the Cross to pay the penalty that we deserve for our sins. If we reject that perfect, unmerited, excruciating, and all-sacrificing gift from a loving God, how can we expect to claim any other blessing?

I say this not only for the unbeliever. We who have already accepted Christ must continue to surrender everything to Him time and time again. We must be fully surrendered to Him always. And He will empower us to see our individual depression and mania as He sees it. Surrender everything to Jesus and He will open your mind, heart, soul, and spirit to receive the unique blessings inherent in your version of bipolar disorder.

And how does one go about this surrender to Christ? Here is a prayer for you to sample:

> "Jesus, you are my God and I am a sinner. I am sorry and I ask you to be my Savior. I deserved to die on that Cross, but you went there in my place and gave me eternal life. I, now, surrender my life to you. Take control of me, Lord. You are my Savior and I celebrate your complete, sovereign authority over me. Jesus, you are my King. Hallelujah! Come live in me. Jesus, I rejoice to surrender all to you."

And when you have finished that prayer - or a surrender prayer of your own word-craft – go nuts praising Him. Then, quietly dwell with Him, whispering His Name in the reverence of your spirit. Just be with Him without thinking and doing. He is there with you. Be there with Him. You are – _right now_ – seated by God in the heavenly realms with Christ.

(Ephesians 2:6) Yes, even _now_. Be there. And live _that_ life here.

2. If you are not already in treatment, for goodness sake, see a Doctor! I have an appointment with my psychiatrist three days from today, February 17, 2008, and I will have many more. If your doctor prescribes medication, try it – every day – for six weeks. Give it a chance to work. Know that I will be taking meds right along with you. Zoloft and Lamictal everyday for the rest of my life. Your body can greatly limit many of the possible side-effects if you give it some time to adjust. And what have you got to lose? How well were things really going before you started the medication?

If your doctor recommends counseling, try it for more than a few sessions. Give yourself and the counselor a chance to get to know each other. I have been a psychotherapist _and_ a therapy patient. I know that counselor and counselee don't always hit it off right from the start. But you're not looking for a buddy. You're looking for somebody with expertise and experience regarding bipolar who will respect what you have to say and tell you the truth – even when you don't want to hear it.

If you do not like something about your treatment for bipolar, let your doctor and counselor know specifically what it is that you do not like. It is your treatment and you are the boss, but please try to be the kind of boss whom you would like to have over you.

If you are taking medication and it is not having the desired effect, tell your doctor! Some medications work for one person who has bipolar, but not for another. There are many that can be tried and I have tried a bunch – Zoloft, effexor, imipramine, elavil, trilafon, lithium, depakote, lamictal, seroquel. And more. Work with your doctor and find the one(s) that are right for you.

Some people who have bipolar disorder are treated with more than one medication at a time. I have been treated variously over the years with anti-depressants, mood-stabilizers, and anti-psychotics. (Don't get wigged-out by the word 'psychotic.' Anti-psychotic drugs just helped to clear my thinking. When I first started taking one, I could not believe how irrational I had been before the drug enabled me to think straight. I did not like the idea of taking an anti-psychotic, but I needed it and it helped.) I was once prescribed depakote, Zoloft, and seroquel all at the same time. I stayed on the seroquel too long, but it did help, and I'm still here to tell about it.

3. Make use of the supports available to you.

It took me about 18 years to learn this one. Supports are not just your doctor and your counselor. Supports include the psych emergency room, mobile crisis teams, the Americans with Disabilities Act, Social Security Disability Benefits, Respite Care, Case Managers, Social Workers, day treatment, group therapy, church groups, ministers, priests, self-help groups like Emotions Anonymous or Alcoholics Anonymous, the Family Medical Leave Act, the National Alliance for the Mentally Ill, your friends, and family. *(Try not to lean too hard on those last two. They are friends and family. They are not doctors, counselors, and psychologists. They cannot be both.)* These services were made for you and me. You have, in all likelihood, contributed your hard-earned tax dollars for their very existence. These people want to help you. They have been trained to help you. They are paid to help you. Let them.

4. Seek God in Every Circumstance. Praise Him at all times. And Proclaim, "I am Blessed."

The Word of God says, "You will seek me and you will find me when you seek me with all your heart." (Jeremiah 29:13) Go after God hard with every ounce of your bipolar being and you <u>will</u> know Him – and there is nothing or no one better. Know Him and you will be transformed in the image of His Son.

"The joy of the Lord is (your) strength." (Nehemiah 10:8c) When you praise God, you bring Him joy and He strengthens you. He is always worthy and you were made to do it. Always. You were perfectly created for doing the act of worship. (<u>Giglio</u>, 2003, p.11, <u>Warren</u>, 2002, p.63) Hallelujah! Do it and be blessed.

Are we really blessed in all things at all times?

Read the first chapter of Job. No man in all of history was ever more terribly devastated than Job. Job lost everything that mattered and more. Family, friends, children, home, fortune, and physical health.

And how did Job respond to his massive, unbearable suffering?

> "Naked came I out of my mother's womb, and naked shall I return thither: the LORD gave, and the LORD hath taken away; blessed be the name of the LORD." (Job 1:21, KJV)

And Job got to know God more profoundly than he ever could have imagined possible. He was transformed in the very midst of his most grave suffering. He gave glory to God and he was abundantly enriched in every way beyond the measure of his prior devastation.

Yes, we are blessed in all things! I proclaim it, now, and I insist that it is always true!

Seek God in every circumstance.

Praise Him at all times.

And know that you are blessed.

"It's still hard for me to have a clear mind thinking on it. But it's the truth even if it didn't happen."
- The Big Chief (Kesey, 1962, p.13)

"If you want any more, you can sing it yourself."
- Bob Dylan, 1992, singing a song he did not write.

Richard Jarzynka can be contacted through his website: www.bipolarman.org

ABOUT THE AUTHOR

from ENTR'ACTE
"Let us Sing Unto the Lord a New Song"

There's a pulse in Richard
that day and night says
revolution   revolution   revolution

and another
not always heard:

poetry   poetry

rippling through his sleep,
a river pulse.

Heart's fire
breaks the chest almost,
flame-pulse,
revolution:

and if its beat
falter
life itself
shall cease.

Heart's river
living water,
poetry:

and if that pulse
grow faint
fever shall parch the soul, breath
choke upon ashes.
But when their rhythms
mesh
then though the pain of living
never lets up

the singing begins.

>   -Denise Levertov [(from, *To Stay Alive*, 1971) (in <u>Poulin</u>, 1971)]

ENDNOTE

1. The United States Department of Education concluded that St. Thomas University officials began receiving information stating that I have bipolar disorder on March 22, 2001 and March 23, 2001. The Dean of the Law School expelled me immediately and without a hearing on March 23, 2001. However, The Department of Education concluded that there was "insufficient evidence of a violation of Section 504" which "provides that no qualified student with a disability shall be excluded from participation in, be denied the benefits of, or otherwise be subjected to discrimination under any academic program."

2. The Eleventh Circuit Federal Court of Appeals appointed an attorney to represent me in the Oral Argument on Appeal. I had already written and submitted to the Eleventh Circuit the Briefs upon which the Oral Argument was based. In addition to representing me at the Oral Argument, the appointed attorney also wrote and submitted two

Briefs supplemental to those that I had filed. I represented myself without an attorney for every other proceeding and document throughout my complaint to the U.S Department of Education, the cases in the United States District Court, and the Appeal to the Eleventh Circuit.

3. There was one student who alleged in a deposition that she once heard me say, "I'll show you what assault is." What I actually said was, "I don't think you know what assault is." I doubted that she knew the legal definition of the term. You can decide for yourself whether that is justification for an immediate expulsion without any due process.

BIBLIOGRAPHY

Darwin, Charles   (1859) "Origin of Species"
Quoted in Strobel (2004, pp. 55-56)

Dungy, Tony   (2007) "Quiet Strength." with
Nathan Whitaker
Tyndale House Publishers, Inc.
Carol Stream, Illinois

Dylan, Bob   (1965) "Love Minus Zero / No Limit
Album: Bringing it All Back Home
Copyright 1965. Renewed 1993
Special Rider Music

(1973) "Forever Young"
Album: Planet Waves
Ram's Horn Music
Renewed by Ram's Horn Music in 2001

(1980) "What Can I Do for You"
Album: Saved
Special Rider Music

(1981) "Every Grain of Sand"
Album: Shot of Love
Special Rider Music

(1985) "Trust Yourself"
Album: Empire Burlesque

(1992) "Froggie Went
A-Courtin'"
Traditional, arranged by Bob
Dylan
Album: Good As I Been to You
Special Rider Music

(1993) Album: World Gone
Wrong
Liner Notes.
Published by Special Rider
Music
All songs traditional, arranged by
Bob Dylan, except
"Lone Pilgrim," written by B.F.
White & Adger M. Pace.

Eldredge, John   "Wild at Heart" (2001)
Thomas Nelson Publishers
Nashville, Tennessee

Erikson, Erik H. "Childhood and Society" (1950)
Second Edition (1963)
W.W. Norton and Company
New York, New York

Faber, Frederick (1849) "I Worship Thee, Most Gracious God"
Original Title: "I Worship Thee, Sweet Will of God"
in *"Jesus and Mary"* (1849)
Music: ABERGELE, John A. Lloyd, (1873)

Fox, Emmett (1934, 1935, 1938) Copyright by Emmett Fox
"The Sermon on the Mount: *The Key to Success in Life"*
Copyright renewed 1966 by Kathleen Whelan
"The Lord's Prayer: *An Interpretation*
Copyright 1932, 1938 by Emmett Fox
Copyright renewed 1966 by Kathleen Whelan
Harper Collins Publishers
New York, New York 10022
First HarperCollins paperback edition published in 1989

Frankl, Viktor E. "Man's Search for Meaning" (1984)
Washington Square Press publication of POCKET BOOKS, a division of Simon and Schuster, Inc.
New York, New York.
First published in Austria in 1946, under the title "*Ein Psycholog erlebt das Konzentrationslager.*"
This translation first published in 1959 by Beacon Press.

Friedman, Emily (November 21, 2008) "Florida Teen Live-Streams His Suicide Online"
ABC News
http://abcnews.go.com/print?id=6306126

Giglio, Louie (2003) "The Air I Breathe" published by Multnomah publishers
a division of Random House, Inc.
Colorado springs, CO

Hanegraaff, Hank (2004) "The Bible Answer Book"
Published by the J. Countryman division of the Thomas Neslon Book Group.
Nashville, Tennessee 37214

Hatfield, Larry   "Educators Against Darwinism" in *Science Digest* (Winter 1979) quoted in Strobel (2004,31)

Herrera, Mario   (November 14, 2007) "Ill That He Blesses is Our Good" http://biblicalthought.com/blog/ill-that-he-blesses-is-our-good-and-unblest-good-is-ill/

Jennings, Waylon   (1978) "I've Always Been Crazy"
(Shel Silverstein)
Album: I've Always Been Crazy
RCA Records

Kesey, Ken   "One Flew Over the Cuckoo's Nest" (1962)
Viking Press
New York, New York
Reprinted. Paperback. Signet.
The New American Library, Inc.
New York, New York

Knowles, Richard T.   "Human Development and Human Possibility: Erikson in the Light of Heidegger."
University Press of America, Inc.
Lanham, Maryland

Levertov, Denise	(1971) "Entr'acte, 'Let us Sing Unto the Lord a New Song'" From Denise Levertov, *To Stay Alive* © 1971 by Denise Levertov Goodman in Poulin,Jr. (1980, 1975, 1971) p.277-278.
Lewis, C.S.	"Mere Christianity" (1952) Harper Collins 2001 Edition Harper Collins Publishers New York, New York
Mellencamp (Cougar), John	(1983) "Authority Song." Album: Uh-Huh Riva Records
Murray, Edward L.	(1986) "Imaginative Thinking and Human Existence" Duquesne University Press Pittsburgh, PA
Petty, Tom	(1989) "I Won't Back Down" Co-written with Jeff Lynne Album: Full Moon Fever MCA Records, Inc. Universal City, California
Poulin, Jr. A.	(1971) "Contemporary American Poetry" Third Edition

Houghton Mifflin Company
Boston, MA
© 1980, 1975 by Houghton Mifflin Company

Sowell, Thomas — "Republicans and Blacks" (April 10, 2008)
http://www.realclearpolitics.com

Strobel, Lee — (1998) "The Case for Christ"
Published by Zondervan
Grand Rapids, Michigan

Strobel, Lee — (2004) "The Case for a Creator"
Zondervan
Grand Rapids, Michigan

Tozer, A.W. — "The Knowledge of the Holy" (1961)
Harper Collins Publishers
New York, New York

Warren, Rick — (2002) "The Purpose-Driven Life
Zondervan
Grand Rapids, Michigan

Watts, Alan W. — (1951) "The Wisdom of Insecurity."
Pantheon Books, a division of Random House, Inc.
New York, New York

Wells, Ph.D., Jonathan	quoted in Strobel (2004, p. 43)
Wesley, John	in Maxwell (1999) "The 21 Indispensible Qualities of a Leader." Thomas Nelson Publishers Nashville, Tennessee
Yevtushenko, Yevgeny	"Early Illusions" (1967) in Murray, p. 256

Printed in the United States
221687BV00001B/1/P